MYSTERIES OF THE MUMMIES

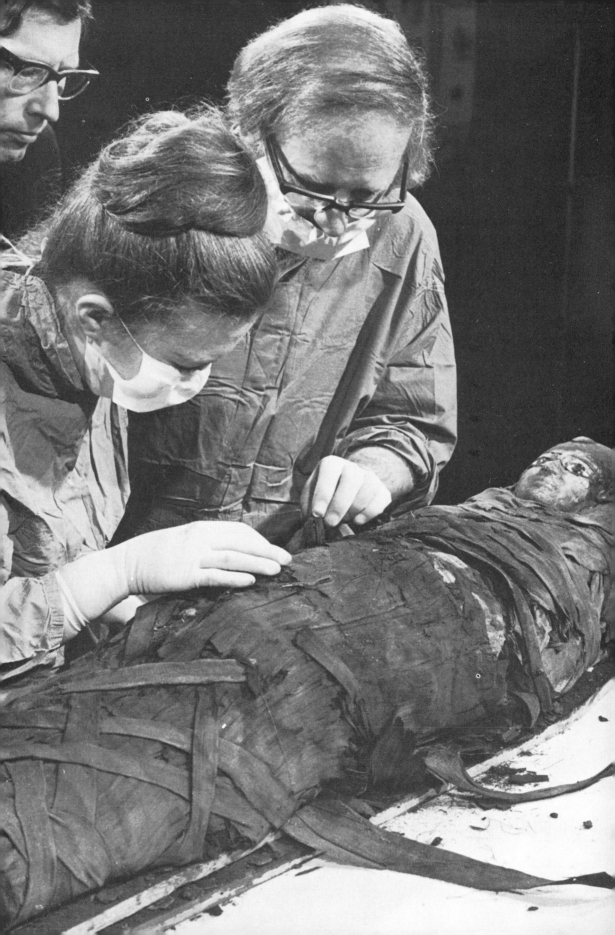

MYSTERIES OF THE MUMMIES

The story of the Manchester University investigation

edited by Dr Rosalie David

BOOK CLUB ASSOCIATES LONDON

First published 1978 by Book Club Associates

Set in Plantin and
printed in Great Britain by Lowe & Brydone Printers Limited
Thetford, Norfolk

Frontispiece: The preliminary examination of mummy 1770

Contents

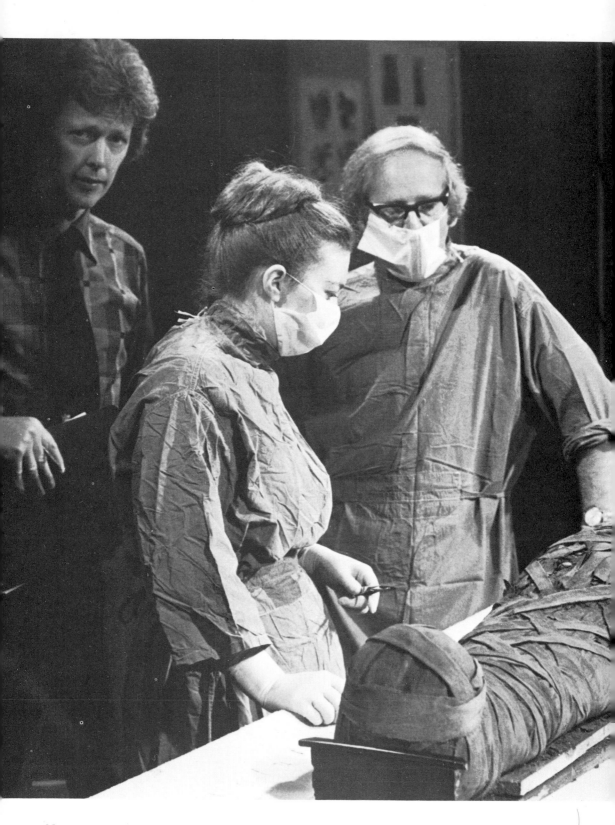

Mummy 1770 on the operating table with Dr Rosalie David and two members of the team of investigat

Prologue

AT 10.30 AM ON THURSDAY, 10 JUNE 1975, in the operating-
theatre at Manchester University Medical School, the rapt
attention of a large and expectant audience was focused on a
group of green-gowned figures clustered round the operating-
table. The TV arc lights picked them out with brilliant clarity. An
operation was about to begin. But this was no ordinary operation
for the 'patient' was already dead. Dead and indeed buried. How
then did he (or she, we cannot be certain which) come to be
lying on an operating-table in the Medical School, thousands of
miles from his (or her) original home, and perhaps more
significantly, thousands of years after the original burial? For the
patient was an Egyptian mummy, name unknown, referred to
prosaically as No 1770, from the collection in Manchester
Museum. The occasion – the unwrapping of a mummy – was a
fairly rare event even in Egyptology. The last time it had taken
place in Manchester was in 1906 when another lady Egyptologist,
the late Dr Margaret Murray, unwrapped the mummies of the
Two Brothers, still on display in the museum. Nearly seventy
years later history was repeating itself, with Dr Rosalie David
and a team of experts from other fields about to unwrap the
anonymous mummy No 1770. The story of that unwrapping and
of the wide range of scientific techniques used in the
investigation which followed, form the subject of this book,
written by the team who carried out this exacting but exciting
task.

However, the unwrapping of 1770 was only the key-event of a
major investigation of the seventeen human and twenty-two
animal mummies in the Egyptology collection at Manchester
Museum. It provided the climax to several years of painstaking
research and investigation by the Manchester team in the most
extensive examination of its kind to have been carried out in
Britain.

Although all the mummies, apart from 1770, were investigated as thoroughly as possible by non-destructive methods of

7

examination, the three which were to prove most interesting were the mummies of Asru, a chantress of Amun, who probably came from Luxor in Upper Egypt, and of the Two Brothers, Khnum Nakht and Nekht Ankh, who came from Rifeh in Middle Egypt, and were the earliest mummies in the Museum's collection.

The project had two basic aims. We wanted to find out as much information as possible from a specific group of Egyptian mummies which could be related to existing knowledge of religious and funerary customs, living conditions, the state of physical and dental health, and the process of mummification in ancient Egypt. We also hoped to find in the bodies evidence of disease which could be identified and, in addition, possible causes of death. Secondly, it was intended to establish a methodology, using many different techniques under near-ideal conditions, for the examination of a group of Egyptian mummified remains, which other institutions could adopt and adapt for the investigation of their own collections.

The study of the investigation is resumed in Chapter 4. In Chapters 1, 2, and 3 an attempt is made to provide some of the background against which the events described must be seen.

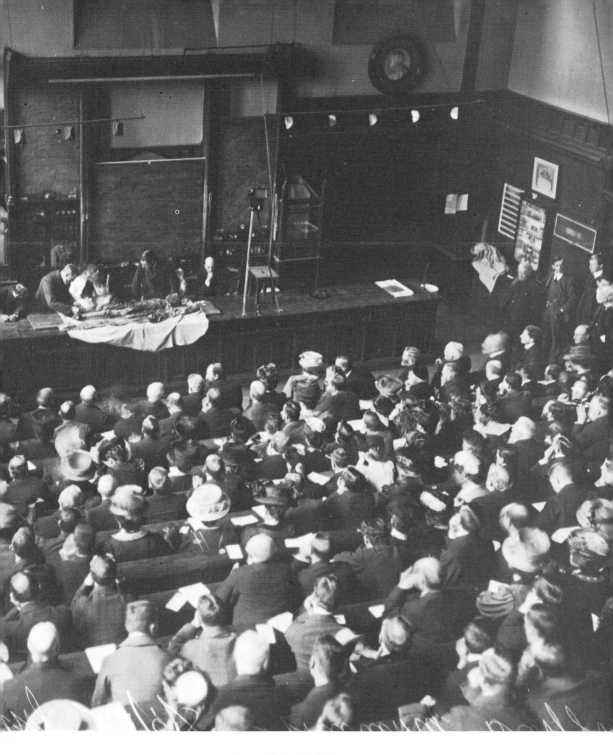

Above left: Dr Margaret Murray and members of her team before unwrapping one of the Two Brothers at Manchester University in 1906

Above: The scene in the lecture hall as an invited audience watches Dr Murray dissecting this mummy

Part I
THE BACKGROUND

Above: The famous group of pyramids at Giza
Previous pages: A view across the Nile, life source of Egypt,
with the Theban hills in the background

1 The Geography and History of Ancient Egypt

THREE DEGREES SOUTH OF THE EQUATOR, in the region of the Great Lakes, rises Africa's longest river, the Nile. In its upper course it is known as Bahr el-Jebel or Mountain Nile; then from below its junction with the Bahr el-Ghazel it is known as the White Nile. At Khartoum the White Nile is joined by the Blue Nile, which rises in Lake Tana in the highlands of Ethiopia. Just north of Khartoum the river enters the region of Nubian sandstone through which it winds a tortuous course, describing a huge S-bend before it enters Egypt proper at the First Cataract, just south of Elephantine. Between Khartoum and Aswan there are six cataracts – places where the river has failed to cut a perfect channel through the stone and the stream is obstructed by scattered, irregular piles of rock. At none of the cataracts, however, is there a well-marked and considerable fall, a proper waterfall, as such. The rock interferes with navigation most seriously in the region of the Fourth, Second, and First Cataracts. Near Elephantine the Nile passes the granite barrier of the First Cataract and thereafter pursues an uninterrupted course northward to the Mediterranean.

West of the river stretches the Libyan Desert with its seemingly endless desolate hills of sand, gravel, and rock from 650 to 1,000 foot high. This otherwise waterless expanse is broken by an irregular chain of oases which runs roughly parallel with the river. East of the Nile lies the Eastern or 'Arabian' Desert, a rather less inhospitable region that affords a bare subsistence to wandering nomads and their animals. At Edfu, about seventy miles north of Elephantine, the underlying sandstone is replaced by limestone which affords the Nile an easier task in the erosion of its bed. West of the river, near Asyut, the Bahr Yusef (Joseph's river), a minor channel some 200 miles long, leaves the main stream and flows into the fertile depression known as the Fayum.

Egypt proper comprises the territory between the First Cataract and the Mediterranean, 550 miles to the north. It divides

A tomb painting showing wildfowling and fishing in the marshes of the Delta

naturally into two regions, the Valley and the Delta. The Valley, the passage which the Nile has forced from Central Africa to the Mediterranean, is a corridor some 500 miles long and from six to twelve miles wide, although in places it narrows down to the actual breadth of the river. On either side, steep, bare walls of rock rise 650 foot or more up to the level of the flanking deserts. In the Valley, the Nile flows northward through a uniformly flat plain, across an unbroken expanse of fields and pastures. In many places the red and yellow desert sands drift over the cliffs and often invade the green fields so that it is possible to stand with one foot in the green of the Valley and one foot in the desert sand. Overhead the sun shimmers in a clear blue sky, only occasionally marked by passing clouds. From the north may come a draught of refreshing wind. This is Upper Egypt, the land that the ancient Egyptians called *Ta-Shema*.

North of the ancient Memphis (present-day Cairo) the appearance of the country changes abruptly. The cliffs of the Eastern and Western Deserts diverge and the Valley spreads out like a gigantic fan into a delta nearly 100 miles long and nearly 200 miles across the curving northern perimeter, a vast area of low-lying plain stretching away to the distant sea. Here land, lagoons, canals, and beaches merge in one level surface; and here the brilliance of the sun is veiled by a transparent haze and the heat is tempered by humidity. This is Lower Egypt, the Delta, known to the ancient Egyptians as *Ta-Meh*, the northern

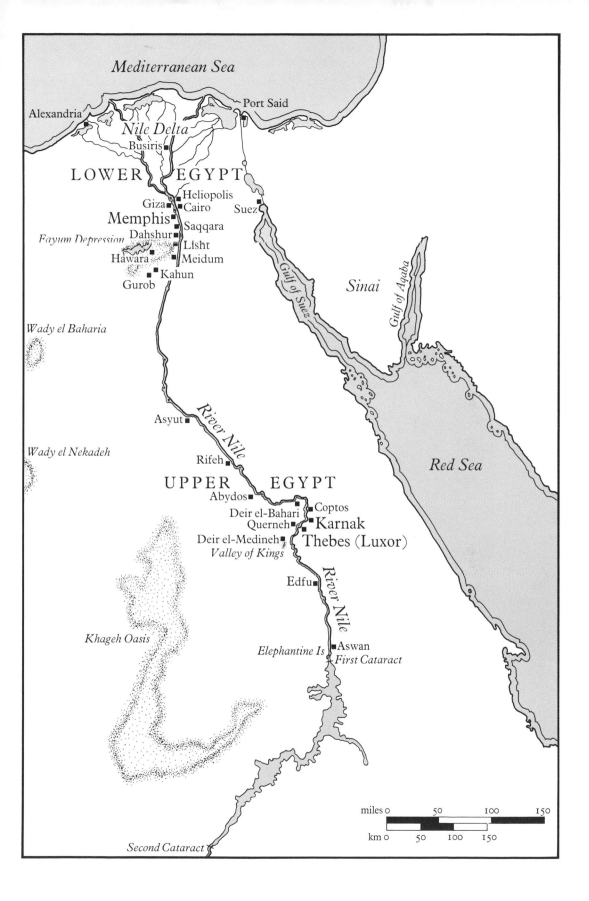

Mediterranean Sea

Alexandria

Nile Delta

Port Said

Busiris

LOWER EGYPT

Heliopolis

Giza Cairo

Suez

Memphis

Saqqara

Fayum Depression

Dahshur

Lisht

Hawara

Meidum

Kahun

Gurob

Wady el Baharia

Gulf of Suez

Sinai

Gulf of Aqaba

Red Sea

Asyut

River Nile

Wady el Nekadeh

Rifeh

UPPER EGYPT

Abydos

Coptos

Deir el-Bahari

Querneh

Karnak

Deir el-Medineh

Thebes (Luxor)

Valley of Kings

Edfu

River Nile

Khageh Oasis

Elephantine Is

Aswan

First Cataract

miles 0   50   100   150

km 0   50   100   150

Second Cataract

land. 'Away from the heat and solitude of the African desert, it is in touch with the busy roads of the Mediterranean, it is attached to the Arabian isthmus, it reaches out towards Europe, and it is refreshed by the sweet breezes of the North,' (A. Moret, *The Nile and Egyptian Civilization*, London, 1927, pp 26-7).

Although the differences between the Valley and the Delta, the Two Lands as the Egyptians called them, are great enough to have made a marked impression on the history of Egypt, the regions are nevertheless inseparable from each other. 'They harmonize together; the Valley is all length, the Delta all breadth, but their cultivable surface, their economic value, their population, are equal, and the two equal forces balance one another,' (A. Moret). The two Egypts could never prosper apart. The Delta by itself lacks the resources of the country above. 'Cut off from the Valley, the Delta could no more live than a flower in full bloom shorn from the slender stalk which feeds it.' On the other hand, the Valley without the coast is a blind alley with no outlet on Europe or Asia. 'Without the Delta the Valley would be a stalk with no flower blooming at the end.' What unites the Two Lands is the Nile: without it Egypt would simply be part of the great deserts on either side of the river.

The rainfall of Egypt is, and was, negligible; only the Delta, and then only its northern part, lies within reach of the winter rains of the Mediterranean. In Upper Egypt rain is exceptional and when it does occur it comes in short but violent downpours that often do more harm than good. Agriculture in Egypt was and is entirely dependent on the Nile. The cultivable land of Egypt consists of black alluvial soil deposited by the river over many thousands of years. In the often-quoted words of Hecataeus, Egypt is literally 'the gift of the Nile'.

The most important natural event of the year in Egypt was the annual inundation, when the river, swollen by rain falling on the highlands of Ethiopia, rose, flooded its banks, and spread over the fields, depositing on them a layer of fertile silt brought down by the waters. The Nile's rise was noticeable by the beginning of July when the river became greenish with a vegetable scum from the equatorial waters. A fortnight or so later muddy silt began to arrive, imparting a reddish tinge to the water. As the flood swelled and reached the level of the surrounding fields the dykes would be breached and the waters would cover the land to a depth of several feet. By September the villages, each protected by dykes, stood like islands amid a vast shining expanse of water which stretched from one side of the Valley to the other; dotted here and there were trees and isolated houses. Then the water would begin to subside and by the end of October the Nile would again be between its own banks. By

The pyramid of Chephren at Giza showing a mastaba in the foreground. Members of the Pharaoh's court were buried in these at the foot of his pyramid

the end of the following May it would be a shrunken stream kept alive only by the more constant flow of the White Nile from the Great Lakes region of East Africa. The earth would now be dry and cracked under the scorching rays of the sun. Then the cycle would begin all over again.

As soon as the waters of the inundation receded from the land, ploughing and sowing began. The consciousness of Egypt's dependence upon the inundation is reflected throughout her history and appears in the earliest religious texts that have survived, the so-called 'Pyramid Texts', inscribed in certain Fifth and Sixth Dynasty pyramids at Saqqara: 'Those who see the Nile when it surges tremble, the meadows laugh, and the river-banks are inundated. The gods' offerings descend, the faces of men are bright, the hearts of the gods rejoice,' (R. O. Faulkner, *The Ancient Egyptian Pyramid Texts*, Oxford, 1969).

But although the Nile rose with unfailing regularity it was temperamental, and the height of the inundation varied from year to year. A very low Nile could be disastrous, bringing with it the spectre of famine and disease. On the wall of the temple causeway of the pyramid of the Pharaoh Unas (Fifth Dynasty) at Saqqara is a relief depicting a group of starving people, some of them so weak that they have to be supported. In texts from the Sixth Dynasty onwards there are a number of references to famine and its effects. An abnormally high inundation, however, could be an equally terrible menace, for unless controlled the flood could drown land, villages, and even towns. Such a disaster occurred as recently as 1874 when considerable loss of both human and animal life, as well as crops and property, was caused by exceptional floods. In Egyptian texts, however, the evil effects of a high Nile, like other disasters are rarely dwelt upon, the emphasis being almost entirely on the favourable aspects of a high inundation.

Very early in their history the Egyptians appreciated the need to undertake measures to control and regulate the Nile waters, and over the centuries there evolved the complex and highly effective system of irrigation known as the 'basin' system, which continued in use throughout Egypt until about the middle of the last century. Under this system the land was divided by strong earth banks into compartments or 'basins' of varying sizes. The banks ran parallel to the river and as near to it as possible, with cross banks between them and the desert edge, thus giving the area covered a chequer board appearance. When the Nile rose, water was let into the basins through canals, flooding the land, and was held there while it deposited silt. After the river had fallen sufficiently, the water was drained off again and cultivators followed the retreating waters and sowed their crops.

The Nile at Aswan showing the narrow strip of cultivation giving way to sand dunes

Above and opposite: From earliest times agriculture in the Nile valley required
considerable organization. These tomb paintings show scribes recording
the gathering of the harvest and men bringing in a basket of wheat

The construction, extension, and maintenance of the irrigation system required a complex organization and considerable resources, human and material. It is a moot point whether it was the advent of a strong centralized state in the First Dynasty that made large-scale irrigation measures possible, or whether it was the cooperation and communal effort required to extend and enlarge small-scale projects that provided a stimulus towards the growth of a central authority. What is clear, however, is the importance which the pharaohs attached to the building of dams and dykes and the digging of canals, and to their maintenance.

Although the climate of Egypt has undergone no basic change since dynastic times, there have been great environmental changes. In antiquity the Nile Valley in Upper Egypt was fringed on either side by a belt of marshes and swamps, the width varying in different localities. Here papyrus, lotus, and other aquatic plants grew in abundance. In the Delta papyrus swamps covered vast areas. This dense, green world sheltered a varied fauna: brightly-coloured water-birds of all kinds, crocodiles, cobras, hippopotamuses, and the sacred ibis, while in the deserts roamed lions, leopards, wild cattle, ostriches, gazelles, and other creatures which have long since retreated further south.

An historical outline

The long history of Egypt is divided into thirty-one dynasties, following the scheme of Manetho, an Egyptian priest, who wrote a history of Egypt (in Greek) around 250 BC. For greater convenience these dynasties are grouped into a smaller number of periods, shown in the table below, together with the preceding and succeeding non-dynastic periods:

Pre-dynastic period   c. 5000-3100 BC
Archaic period (Dyn. I and II)   3100-2686 BC
Old Kingdom (Dyn. III-VI)   2686-2181 BC
First Intermediate period (Dyn. VII-XI)   2181-1991 BC
Middle Kingdom (Dyn. XII)   1991-1786 BC
Second Intermediate period (Dyn. XIII-XVII)   1786-1552 BC
New Kingdom (Dyn. XVIII-XX)   1552-1069 BC
Third Intermediate period (Dyn. XXI-XXVI)   1069-525 BC
Late period (Dyn. XXVII-XXXI)   525-332 BC
Conquest by Alexander the Great   332 BC
Period of Greek rule (Ptolemaic period)   332-30 BC
Roman Period   30 BC-AD 641
Islamic conquest AD 641

The three greatest periods of Egyptian history are, as their names imply, the Old, Middle, and New Kingdoms, and these will receive most attention in the following relatively brief outline of Egyptian history. The period before Dynasty I is known as the Pre-dynastic period, and this will be considered first, though briefly.

THE PRE-DYNASTIC PERIOD (*c.* 5000-3100 BC) On the evidence of Carbon-14 dating, farming developed in Egypt some time between 5200 and 4000 BC. The peoples involved fall into two geographical groups, one in Lower Egypt, the Delta, and one in Upper Egypt, the Nile Valley proper. Only in Upper Egypt is there a well-established chronological sequence leading up to Dynasty I, with the periods as follows: Tasian, Badarian, Nagada I, and Nagada II. The Tasian and Badarian people, like the peoples of Lower Egypt, practised mixed farming and lived mainly on spurs overlooking the Valley. It was only in the following Nagada I period that people moved down and settled in the fertile Valley itself. In the Nagada II period there is evidence of increasing contact with the rest of the Near East, painted pottery and copper metalwork, axes, daggers, and knives being the principal forms. By late Nagada II times the separate villages and communities had developed into two groups or kingdoms, one in the Delta region and one in Upper Egypt. It was the unification of these two kingdoms under one ruler by the first king of Dynasty I (Menes) that marks the beginning of Egyptian history. The union is commemorated by the Pharaoh's titles, Lord of the Two Lands, King of Upper and Lower Egypt, which were a permanent part of the royal titles down to the end of dynastic times nearly 3,000 years later.

ARCHAIC PERIOD AND OLD KINGDOM (Dyn. I-VI) The Old Kingdom is noted above all else for the pyramids, possibly the most spectacular monuments ever erected. About eighty in all were built in the Nile Valley. The pyramid form seems to have developed out of the mastaba, a type of tomb in use from Dynasty I onwards. The word mastaba is Arabic for 'bench' and was applied to these tombs because their remains resembled, on a large scale, the simple bench outside present-day Egyptian houses. In pre-dynastic times the dead were buried in a simple pit in the ground and covered by a mound of sand for greater protection. Sand, however, is unsatisfactory as a permanent covering and by Dynasty I kings and nobles were buried beneath substantial mastabas of mud brick. These were rectangular in plan and divided internally into as many as thirty cells or chambers for the storage of all the domestic and other equipment which the dead man would need in the after-life. Almost certainly the mastaba was a simplified representation of the contemporary house, with such things as doors and corridors omitted because the spirit of the dead man was presumed to be able to move freely from room to room through the walls. Beneath this superstructure was the burial pit or chamber, dug into the ground and protected, in theory at least, by the elaborate structure above. During Dynasties II and III, for greater security, the mastaba superstructure became a solid mass of stone rubble faced with brick, the system of storage chambers being transferred below ground. All these precautions, however, failed to defeat the tomb robbers and in Dynasties V and VI the mastaba superstructure was composed of columned halls and chambers, again recalling the houses of the living, and elaborately decorated in relief sculpture with scenes from the owner's life.

Although mastabas continued as tombs for the nobility, in Dynasty III the pyramid appeared for the first time as a royal tomb, albeit in stepped form. King Zoser was buried at Saqqara in what, in its final form, was a step-pyramid with six stages. Even this, however, started life as a mastaba, square in plan (205 by 205 foot), and about 25 foot high. This was enlarged to 233 foot square, and then to a rectangle 251 by 233 foot. A further enlargement made it 280 by 252 foot, by which time it was the lowest stage of a stepped pyramid 140 foot high. All these

The step pyramid of
Zoser and part of the
complex surrounding it

changes seem to have taken place in quick succession, but there
were still more changes to come. The plan was extended again,
making it 410 by 360 foot, and the whole structure was
eventually completed as a six-step pyramid, 195 foot high.
Beneath this pyramid superstructure was a rectangular shaft 23
foot square, sunk to a depth of 92 foot into the rock, with the
tomb chamber at the bottom.

The step-pyramid of Zoser was the first of the long series of
pyramids built during the Old and Middle Kingdoms, in step
form and later in true pyramid form. It was early in Dynasty IV
that the transition was made from the step to the true pyramid.
The name of Sneferu, first king of the dynasty, is associated with
no less than three pyramids, two at Dahshur and one at Meidum,
although it seems unlikely that all three are actually his. The
Meidum pyramid started as a seven-step structure; it was then
heightened by 45 foot and an additional step was added. The
final alteration was the filling-in of the steps and the covering of

24

the whole structure with a smooth facing of limestone, transforming it into a true pyramid. The two pyramids at Dahshur appear to have been conceived from the beginning as true pyramids, although only one was completed as such. The so-called Bent Pyramid (620 foot square) inclines inwards at a shallower angle about halfway up and is possibly the result of hasty and economical completion. The second pyramid at Dahshur is, in fact, the first to be both started and completed as a geometrically true pyramid. It is notable for the relatively shallow angle of its sides, very similar to the upper position of the Bent Pyramid.

The achievement of the true pyramid was followed in Dynasties IV, V, and VI by a whole series of magnificent pyramids, including those at Giza which, in the words of I. E. S. Edwards, are 'possibly the most celebrated group of monuments in the world'. The pyramids of Cheops, Chephren, and Mycerinus at Giza represent the main work of Dynasty IV. The three pyramids, and the Sphinx, formed part of a great necropolis or cemetery consisting of dozens of mastabas, the burial places of the nobles who wished to be near the royal tombs. The pyramids of Dynasties V and VI were much smaller than those of the Giza group but like them conformed to what may be regarded as a regular plan. The pyramid is, in fact, only one element in a whole complex of associated buildings. These consist of the valley temple, the causeway, the funerary temple, the pyramid enclosure, and the small subsidiary pyramids to house close relatives, such as the wives and daughters of the Pharaoh.

THE MIDDLE KINGDOM (DYN. XII) After the end of Dynasty VI, during the First Intermediate period, there was anarchy for nearly a century and a half in Egypt when centralized government broke down and most of the monuments just described were ravaged and destroyed by tomb robbers. Only in the second half of Dynasty XI was there a return to more settled conditions under three kings, all named Mentuhotep. The first of these, Nebhepetre-Mentuhotep, built an unusual funerary temple at Deir el-Bahari, incorporating a small pyramid and a rock-cut burial chamber situated beneath the cliff against which the temple was placed. This was quite unlike anything that had gone before and, like Zoser's step-pyramid, must be regarded as an original architectural concept. The principal kings of Dynasty XII, one of the greatest dynasties in Egyptian history, were Amenemmes I, II, and III and Sesostris I, II, and III, all of whom built pyramids on more or less conventional lines. One of the best preserved is that of Sesostris I, second king of the dynasty, at Lisht. The pyramid itself, 352 foot square and 200 foot high, stood within a double enclosure with most of the subsidiary pyramids between the inner and outer walls. The later kings of Dynasty XII used brick instead of stone for the inner core of their pyramids. A few pyramids were built during the Second Intermediate period but this form of burial was abandoned at the beginning of Dynasty XVIII and of the New Kingdom.

Apart from royal burials in pyramids, the burial practice for Middle Kingdom nobles and officials included both mastabas and rock-cut tombs. The main use of the mastaba tomb was in Dynasties I-VI, but even in Middle Kingdom times some court officials were still buried in mastabas near the royal pyramids. However, increasing use was made of rock-cut tombs. This practice had begun in the latter part of the Old Kingdom but only in the Middle and New Kingdoms was it used on a large scale. Use was made of the cliff faces found in many places close to the Nile. Instead of a mastaba superstructure containing a pillared hall and chambers, the whole complex was dug out of the solid rock, with a shaft or passage leading down to the actual burial place. As in mastabas, the walls were decorated with scenes and inscriptions illustrating the occupant's life, either carved in relief or painted. Externally there was often an elaborate architectural facade. In some cases there were external buildings as well, such as valley temples, following pyramid practice.

The new strength of Egypt during the Middle Kingdom sprang from the dynamic qualities of the rulers and their ability to centralize power once again in the hands of the king. Egypt renewed contact with Nubia to the south, and with Asia Minor. A more aggressive group of people had entered Nubia, and to restore her domination of the region and to regain access to the gold and hard building stone, the Egyptians had to pursue a policy of force. They built a string of fortresses in the south, garrisoned by Egyptians whose presence ensured the safe passage of boats to and from Nubia and gradually subdued the surrounding population.

With the peoples of Asia Minor, the Egyptians pursued a non-aggressive policy; contacts were re-established and trade flourished. Egyptian tomb decorations show the arrival in Egypt of foreign peoples bearing goods. Relationships existed with the people from the isles of the Aegean, from Byblos on the Phoenician coast, and elsewhere. Egypt also traded with Punt – the land from which incense was acquired – which may have been situated on the Red Sea coast, perhaps in the region of present-day Somaliland.

THE NEW KINGDOM (DYN. XVIII-XX) Between the Middle and New Kingdoms are the five dynasties, XIII-XVII, of the Second Intermediate Period (1786-1552 BC), some of which may in fact be contemporary with each other, one dynasty ruling in Lower Egypt and one in Upper Egypt. Two of these dynasties are those of the Hyksos, Asiatic settlers in the Delta who gradually took political control and extended their influence, if not their direct rule, over much of Egypt. The end of the Hyksos domination and the Second Intermediate period came with the growing power of the Dynasty XVII princes of Thebes in Upper Egypt, who claimed authority over the whole of the country. Eventually they were successful and the Hyksos were defeated, c. 1552 BC, by Amosis, founder of Dynasty XVIII and the New Kingdom.

During the early part of Dynasty XVIII, the Egyptians radically changed their foreign policy. Previously they had shown little interest in attempting to impose their rule on other peoples, provided that access to the commodities found in neighbouring areas was not impeded. They preferred to trade with their neighbours rather than to fight them.

However, after the expulsion of the Hyksos the Egyptians started to expand their horizons, partly to prevent another invasion of their country by outsiders. During the New Kingdom, and particularly Dynasty XVIII, their kings led expeditions to subdue the petty independent cities and states established in the region of Palestine and to bring them under Egyptian influence. The Egyptians successfully fought the Mitannians and the Hittites in Asia Minor, who, at different times, each posed a threat to Egypt's dominance of the area.

The result was the first Empire; later Empires, under the Assyrians, Persians, and Greeks, were larger and more firmly organized, but the Egyptians controlled an area which stretched from Nubia to the River Euphrates. Within it, native governors loyal to Egypt were appointed to rule over cities and states in a loose confederation. The booty brought back from these expeditions and the continuing tribute paid by vassal states ensured the wealth of Egypt and particularly of Amun, great God of Thebes, and his priesthood at Karnak, to whom many offerings were made.

In Dynasty XVIII royal burial in pyramids was finally abandoned. The pyramid superstructure was too clear an indication of a rich burial and too much of an attraction for tomb robbers. In the New Kingdom the opposite approach was adopted – that of concealing the burial so that there was no surface indication that it existed. The site chosen for the royal tombs was a remote valley in the western hills behind Thebes, and there the kings of Dynasties XVIII, XIX, and XX were buried

Previous pages:
The pyramid of Chephren with part of the surrounding necropolis

in rock tombs cut deep into the heart of the mountain. There were no subsidiary buildings immediately associated with these tombs, as in the case of the pyramids, since this would have betrayed the location of the burial. The funerary temples were built in the Nile Valley itself, at the edge of the cultivation zone on the far side of the intervening mountain.

Over sixty rock-cut tombs are known in the Valley of the Kings, the earliest being that of Tuthmosis I, third king of Dynasty XVIII. No two tombs are identical but most of them incorporate the same general range of features. From the entrance a series of alternating staircases and descending passages leads deep into the mountain. In some corridors a deep shaft occupied the full width, to make access difficult for robbers and to drain off any surface water running down into the tomb. In some cases there are also side chambers opening off the corridors. At the end of this system of corridors and staircases there is the suite of rooms, usually including at least one pillared hall, which formed the tomb proper. The tomb of Ramesses III (second king, Dynasty XX) was tunnelled some 300 foot into the rock and among a number of chambers, included two pillared halls. The innermost, with eight pillars, measured 60 by 36 foot and contained the sarcophagus; there were smaller chambers associated with it. The tomb of Queen Hatshepsut (fifth ruler, Dynasty XVIII), by far the longest of all rock tombs, is cut nearly 700 foot into the mountain, and descends over 300 foot. Many of the corridor and chamber walls of these tombs are decorated with relief sculpture and texts illustrating the king's journey through the underworld, and were intended to help him on his way.

In spite of these elaborate precautions the plundering of royal tombs continued, and none of the funerary equipment of the many great kings of Dynasties XVIII, XIX, and XX has been found. What did escape the tomb robbers, except for some very minor interference, was the tomb of Tutankhamun, twelfth king of Dynasty XVIII. Tutankhamun reigned for only nine years and was still very young when he died. Compared with most other tombs in the Valley of the Kings his tomb was small and he was not, in fact, historically a very important king. Tutankhamun's importance to us lies in the fact that his grave and all his burial equipment were found virtually intact. The sheer richness and splendour of this, the burial of a minor king, makes one wonder how much more rich and splendid must have been the burials of the truly great rulers of the New Kingdom, such as Tuthmosis III (sixth king, Dynasty XVIII), or Ramesses III (second king, Dynasty XX).

The rock-cut tombs in the Valley of the Kings were designed only for the body of the dead king and the offerings made at the time of burial. The funerary temple to perpetuate the king's memory was situated elsewhere, so as not to reveal the tomb's whereabouts. The funerary temples of the New Kingdom were, in fact, on the other side of the mountain from the Valley of the Kings, in the neighbourhood of the modern town of Luxor. Two of the most elaborate are those of Ramesses II and Ramesses III, both built on very much the same lines. In fact, their funerary temples are only part of a complex of buildings within a great enclosure wall which includes also a royal palace, houses for the priests and other officials, and, above all, great batteries of magazines of storage chambers. Perhaps the most unusual funerary temple is that of Queen Hatshepsut whose tomb was mentioned above. She chose a site against the cliffs at Deir el-Bahari, next to the equally unusual funerary temple of the Dynasty XI king Mentuhotep, and built a temple on not dissimilar lines, but without the pyramid. The funerary temples of Ramesses II and III and of Hatshepsut are only three, although perhaps the most spectacular, of a huge range of monuments associated with the Valley of the Kings which stretch for some three miles in the neighbourhood of modern Luxor (ancient Thebes), capital of Egypt during New Kingdom times.

Thebes is also the site of the greatest temple complex in Egypt, at Karnak, just north of Luxor on the east bank of the Nile. The temple as a whole is dedicated to the god Amen-Re, but it incorporates also the cult of Mut, Amun's wife, and of Khons, their son, and in fact, consists of at least a dozen temple buildings, in three separate but linked enclosures. The main

The obelisk of Queen Hatshepsut at the temple of Amun at Karnak

The temple complex at Karnak is the largest area of religious buildings in the world. Started in Dynasty XII it reached its peak in Dynasty XVIII when tribute from Egypt's empire was brought to the state god Amun.
Left: A ram-headed sphinx from the temple of Amun.
Above: The pillars and clerestory lighting of the hypostyle hall of the temple of Amun.
Right: The lotus columns of the entrance court of the temple of Amun

Typical tomb paintings
of everyday scenes
showing the harvest
(top), with cows
trampling the grain,
and people hunting
with boomerangs
in the marshes
of the Delta
(bottom)

temple has a complex structural history covering nearly 2,000 years of additions and alterations, from Middle Kingdom to Roman times, although the bulk of the existing remains are of New Kingdom date, including the justly famous Hypostyle Hall. This hall (330 by 170 foot) contains no less than 134 columns, the twelve largest of which are 64 foot high and 33 foot in circumference and rise above the remaining columns to allow for the admission of light by means of a clerestory.

THE PTOLEMAIC PERIOD (332-30 BC) After Dynasty XX and the end of the New Kingdom the late dynastic period (Dynasties XXI-XXXI) occupies the years 1085-332 BC. Although largely a period of decline it contains one period, the Saite (Dynasty XXVI 664-525 BC), when there was a return to Egypt's former splendour under six kings: Psammetichus I, Necho II, Psammetichus II, Apries, Amasis, and Psammetichus III. Alexander the Great's conquest in 332 BC brought the Egyptian dynastic period to an end and after his death power eventually fell into the hands of the Greek governor, Ptolemy Lagus, who in 305 BC, declared himself king under the name of Ptolemy Soter. The Ptolemaic period embraced twelve rulers named Ptolemy (I-XII), and Cleopatra, whose death in 30 BC brought the Greek dynasty to an end. There followed a long period of Roman rule which was in turn brought to an end by the Mohammedan conquest in AD 641.

2 Social and Religious Life

MOST OF THE PREVIOUS CHAPTER relates to the top level of society, the king and the nobility, but life for the bulk of the population must have been very different, and in many ways, not far removed from present-day conditions.

As early as the Old Kingdom, and probably before this date, the Egyptians had developed a highly organised, hierarchical state which functioned for and around the god-king, and in its social structure resembled a pyramid. The king, believed to be half-divine, was in theory high priest of every temple, the chief justice, head of the army, and the sole owner of Egypt, its people and its contents. He was subject only to Ma'at, the goddess of truth and justice, who maintained the right order of the universe and mankind. In practice, many of his duties were delegated, originally to other members of the royal family but eventually to the increasingly powerful nobles. The vizier – a position established at a very early date – was in most respects the king's deputy and was responsible for the organisation of this highly centralized bureaucracy. The country was probably governed both from a central administration, attached to the king's main residence, and from local centres. Taxes were paid in kind and were stored in great magazines. In the later periods special departments dealt with Egypt's diplomatic contacts with foreign countries, and in the period of the Empire with her government of subordinate peoples.

The upper classes of Egyptian society were mostly engaged in political service to the king, often as scribes – a profession regarded with the highest esteem. Also included were doctors and lawyers, and from the New Kingdom onwards, the highest-ranking officers of the professional army and navy. The priesthood, apart from the full-time temple administrators, consisted of professional men such as lawyers or doctors, who, in addition to their primary profession, held a priesthood of the deity associated with that profession; these men devoted a number of months each year to sacred duties at the temple. The

Bearers carrying food and drink in a funerary procession from a tomb painting of the New Kingdom

37

well-to-do usually also possessed grand estates in the country-side, where their servants tended the fields.

The middle classes consisted of the lower levels of government officials, small land-owners, and craftsmen who by taking on additional work had amassed enough wealth to raise their status. Among these were the goldsmiths and sculptors whose work was in great demand by the great nobles and their ladies.

Then there was the body of craftsmen who were loosely associated in working groups, each under the direction and training of a master craftsman. They were mostly associated with the temples or the court, but could, and often did, carry out private work for individuals. Among the poorer people were the men and women engaged in textile and food manufacture, and in the later periods those who became professional soldiers and sailors.

At the base of this social 'pyramid', however, were the mass of people who can best be described as serfs. Although not strictly

Scenes taken from New Kingdom tombs. Goldsmiths and joiners at work (above left) and musicians entertaining the nobility at a banquet (above right)

in bondage they nevertheless were tied to the tasks of working another man's land. They were also subject to corvée duty, when at the king's behest they could be sent to work on the great building projects, to the mines in Sinai, or to supplement the armed forces. It was from this group that navvies were recruited to build the pyramids of the early kingdoms.

It can be seen that most of these areas would have provided careers or work only for men. In general terms, women were expected to remain at home and to rear their children. Only a very few could read and write, and although the laws safeguarding a woman's status and her legal rights in marriage and divorce were enlightened, nevertheless her position in society was based on her husband's occupation. It is probable that women in the lower social groups in fact had greater freedom to work than did the wives and daughters of professional men. Women of these lower groups were employed in domestic service or in the manufacture of food and textiles,

39

and they might also be engaged in troupes to sing, dance, and entertain the nobility at banquets. They could also become professional mourners, attending the funeral processions of the well-to-do. Although some women were present in the temples as singers and musicians, it is unlikely that they took part in the performance of the god's ritual.

Not a great deal is known about the size and distribution of the population as a whole. Even in the Roman period, when a census was taken every fourteen years, it is not possible to arrive at an accurate figure. Nor is it yet possible to say anything very definite about the average expectation of life in ancient Egypt. On living and working conditions, however, and people's personal and communal habits, much more information is available.

Except on one or two occasions there appears to have been no conscious town-planning in ancient Egypt. The geometrically planned and surveyed town, with rectangular blocks of houses and regular streets at right angles, is an intellectual concept rather than any natural evolution of the primitive village. It could, therefore, only be realized either when there were no existing urban conditions, or when the human elements involved were subject to the plan and power of one man.

However such conditions did occasionally occur. During Dynasty XII, for example, at Kahun, a regular planned town was built to house workmen engaged on the construction of a nearby royal pyramid; and in Dynasty XVIII a village was erected in an arid, isolated valley at Deir el-Medineh to accommodate workers employed on making and decorating the royal tombs in the Valley of the Kings. Normally, however, towns and villages simply grew by accretion and alteration. Thus, Memphis, the ancient capital of Egypt, was an agglomeration of villages, precincts, and defended towns which extended over a distance of some eight miles and was about four miles wide. The whole area, however, was not lined with streets and houses but consisted largely of gardens and fields belonging to various villages, which only gradually merged into a more or less continuous city.

Living conditions within the towns and villages naturally varied according to status and wealth. As far as the mass of the population was concerned the evidence suggests that they lived in small, often closely-packed houses constructed of mud brick, wood, and straw, in conditions very similar to, if not identical with, those found in Egyptian provincial towns and villages at the present day. Houses were continually being added to, amalgamated, partly demolished, partly reconstructed, divided, and partitioned for various reasons, financial and domestic. The

result was a network of narrow streets and courtyards, with blocks of contiguous mud-brick houses, shops, workrooms, gardens, byres, and so on, built round, against, and between one another. Areas of this kind existed in most towns and large villages. As in modern times, shared accommodation resulted in congestion. A remarkable glimpse of the crowded conditions and low living standards of the masses in Egypt is afforded by a census return of the Roman period which shows a man owning a tenth part of a house, itself probably of quite modest dimensions, and in that part no fewer than twenty-six people were living.

Conditions such as these were inevitably a breeding-ground for filth and squalor, and the towns and villages of Egypt were infested by all manner of vermin. Thus in houses in the Dynasty XII workers' town at Kahun, the corners of nearly every room had been tunnelled by rodents, and in efforts to keep them out the holes had been blocked up with stones and rubbish. Remains of rodents were found in abundance in the brickwork of the Dynasty XII fortress-town of Buhen near the Second Cataract. The veneration accorded to the cat and the mongoose in ancient Egypt may perhaps to some extent be a reflection of their value in keeping down vermin. In the absence of actual cats one medical text recommends smearing with cat's grease anything from which it was desired to keep away mice. Eggs of lice (nits) have been found adhering to the hair of mummies, and classical writers on Egypt refer to the priest's practice of shaving the whole body every other day 'in order that no lice or anything else that is foul may infest them'.

A Greek magical papyrus dating from the third century AD contains directions for clearing houses of bugs and fleas, and a section of the Ebers medical papyrus (Dynasty XVIII) is devoted to methods of ridding dwellings of vermin of various kinds:

Soul houses from Middle Kingdom tombs. These give some idea of the domestic architecture of this period

41

fleas, snakes, flies, gnats, and rodents. Included in this section also are two recipes to 'sweeten the smell of the house or clothing'. An illuminating glimpse of the state into which dwellings and other buildings could get is furnished by the appearance in domestic property leases dating from the Roman period, of a clause stipulating that at the expiry of the lease (which ranges in surviving documents from eighteen months to two years), the tenant shall deliver up the premises 'free of filth and dirt of all kind'.

It goes without saying that ordinary domestic flies were present in their millions, and the persistence of these insects was reflected in the institution of a military decoration known as the 'golden fly', which may have been awarded for determination in attack.

The disposal of waste, whether personal, domestic, or industrial, was not a matter with which the average Egyptian greatly concerned himself. It is true that by the beginning of the dynastic period sand-latrines were in use among the nobility, and are found even in tombs as part of the equipment for the hereafter. Despite the existence of such installations, however, the method of disposal was basically no different from earlier times, reliance being placed on exposure to the sun's rays. As far as the majority of the population was concerned, the river or any suitable spot in the vicinity served as a convenience. Much household and town waste was doubtless disposed of by being thrown into the river, and some domestic as well as personal waste was tossed into the street. The bulk of town and domestic refuse, however, found its way on to towering outdoor rubbish-heaps; and these mounds, frequented by scavengers such as dogs, hyenas, and vultures, were a characteristic feature of all towns and villages. Deserted buildings in a town might also be used as rubbish repositories in order to save the labour of conveying it to the rubbish-heaps, particularly if these lay some distance away. Refuse was also tipped into pits.

A feature of every village was the pond, known in Arabic as the *birqa*, originally created by excavations for building material. In spite of the attractive appearance of this pond as depicted in some New Kindom tomb paintings in Thebes, it was in fact an expanse of greenish, stagnant, foul-smelling water which served as a drinking-trough for animals, sometimes as a source of household water; in it children, animals, and ducks swam and relieved themselves. On its surface from time to time bloated animal carcasses might also be seen.

The Egyptian view of the after-life required that the body should be preserved in as lifelike a state as possible and buried in a suitable place, furnished with all the equipment and commodities the deceased had needed while alive, including ample food and drink. The status and character of many of those who engaged in the grisly occupation of embalming, the surroundings and conditions in which they worked, and the nature of the resulting refuse, all combined to guarantee the abundant and constant presence of vermin and filth. Once installed in his 'eternal dwelling', as the tomb was called, the deceased, or rather the food deposited with him, became an immediate target for rodents, which found their way into the tomb through every conceivable crack and crevice. The entire Theban necropolis, for example, was always riddled with rodents.

There can be little doubt that the conditions in which the ancient inhabitants of the Nile Valley lived and worked posed grave potential hazards to their health and well-being. However, it does not necessarily follow that all the worst possibilities were, in fact, realized. There is more than a grain of truth in the remark of one anonymous wit: 'Half the secret of good health is cleanliness; the other half is dirtiness'. The outcome of investigations at present in progress at the University of Manchester and elsewhere may well enable us to obtain a more complete and accurate picture.

Religious life

Religion was central to ancient Egyptian civilization. The sharply contrasting surroundings in which the Egyptians lived must have profoundly affected their view of life and death. Beyond the bright green, fertile belt of the Nile Valley the desert stretched away, representing death and hostility. This environment impressed upon the inhabitants the juxtaposition of life and death and the regular cycle of the land's revival by the inundation. The sun and the river were the dual life-giving forces.

The practice of religion took two very distinct forms in ancient Egypt. There was a state or official religion, centred on the temples and connected with the mythologies and rituals which were the preserve of the priests. Although the ordinary people flocked to see the god's statue paraded outside the temple on festival days, and possibly they prayed in the outer courts of the temples, the state religion played little part in their daily lives; the temples were never centres of community worship and the priests had no pastoral duties.

The state cult consisted of many deities; indeed the Egyptians have often been accused of worshipping an almost unintelligible number of gods and goddesses, whose characteristics are often

Scenes of farming in the realm of Osiris who is enthroned on the right with the goddesses Nephthys and Isis. The deceased stands in the centre garlanded with a vine wreath. From a New Kingdom papyrus of the Book of the Dead

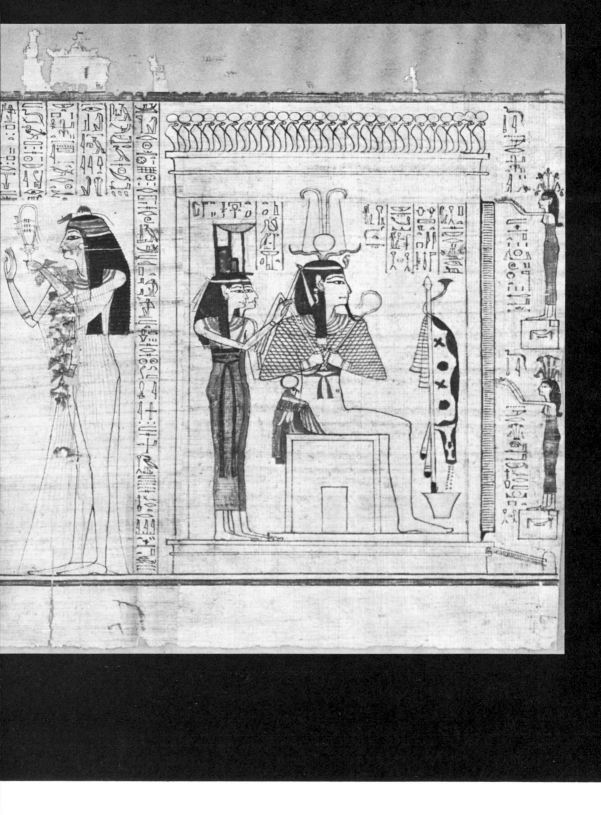

complex and interchangeable. Although the names of many deities have come down to us, it is nevertheless probably wrong to regard the Egyptians as the worshippers of hundreds of deities. Historically, Egypt consisted of many different tribes, each with its own divinity, and when the land became politically united in *c.* 3100 BC many of these deitites were retained in the official pantheon and often their characteristics became merged. However, an individual probably continued throughout Egypt's history to give personal devotion only to his local deity, together with the god's closest associates. The chief state god at any one time was usually the local god of the ruling family who had been raised to prominence by his devotees when they had succeeded in seizing and retaining the throne. In addition, foreign gods brought into Egypt as a result of intercourse with the Nubians to the south and the varied peoples of Asia Minor, were given a place in the Egyptian pantheon. Apart from a brief attempt by Pharaoh Akhenaten at the end of Dynasty XVIII, to introduce a form of solar monotheism, the Egyptians retained an open attitude towards their deities, including any which might provide additional assistance. We are, therefore, left with an indistinct picture of a state cult where most ancient deities of proven worth were retained alongside new divinities. Exclusiveness was virtually absent from Egyptian religion.

However, from time to time the priests attempted to clarify the situation in certain apsects. Deities were thus often grouped in triads – a god, his wife, and their son – and such a family of gods might share a temple. Also certain distinct theologies grew up regarding the creation of the universe and of mankind; these theologies were centred at various cult-cities and they attempted to rival each other in proving the original role of the cult-centre's god in the creating of the universe. These creation theologies attempted to group a number of gods together round the chief deity – thus the Greater and Lesser Enneads (group of nine gods) of Heliopolis and the Ogdoad (group of eight gods) of Hermopolis play important functions in the creation mythology.

From this mass of divinities, however, a small number emerge as extremely important deities in the political and religious development of Egypt.

Horus (the falcon) and Re (the sun god) were both early gods with special royal associations; indeed the increasing importance of Re during the Old Kingdom, at the expense of the king's power, was one of the contributory factors to the eventual disintegration of the Old Kingdom.

In the Middle Kingdom, Osiris – the god of vegetation and ultimately the judge of the underworld and god of the dead – rose to unrivalled pre-eminence. The simple tale of the triumph of good over evil and the promise of salvation and resurrection after death which Osiris promised to his followers, whether rich or poor, guaranteed his cult a place of unrivalled popularity.

With the establishment of the New Kingdom, the warlike and powerful family of Theban princes who gained the throne raised their own local god, Amun, to a position of great power. Associating him with Re, the god of earlier kings, they established Amen-Re, together with Mut, his wife, and Khons, his son, in a great temple at Karnak, the size and magnificence of which was never surpassed. With the growth of Egypt's empire Amen-Re became a supreme god with vast wealth, possessions, and a powerful priesthood.

Perhaps to try to check this power, at the end of Dynasty XVIII King Akhenaten introduced his own form of solar monotheism, of which the symbol was the Aten, or sun's disc. He attempted to make this worship exclusive, disbanding the priests of the other gods, but he failed, and the old many-sided religion was reintroduced in the reign of his half-brother Tutankhamun.

Even the briefest survey of the many state and local gods and goddesses of Egypt would be impossible here, on account of their numbers and complexities. Common to these deities, however, was the need for a 'home' or cult-centre, based on the Egyptian temple.

The Egyptians explained their temples in mythological terms; each temple was regarded as the magical recreation of the original 'Island of Creation' which had arisen from the waters of chaos at the beginning of the world. Here the first shrine was built for the falcon god. Throughout Egypt's long history the temples were all built on the same basic plan with only minor additions and alterations. Their architecture symbolizes the scene at the time of that mythical creation: the ceiling, painted with stars, representing the sky; the floor symbolizing the actual island; the closely-spaced columns surmounted by capitals decorated with carved palm-leaves, palm or lotus flowers, or buds, recreating the island's vegetation; and the sanctuary where the cult-statue was kept symbolizing the original hut-shrine. At the ceremony of consecration, when a new temple was handed over to its resident deity, a special ritual was enacted which magically activated the temple, its wall-reliefs and its statues, and it became, in effect, the original mythical island, a centre of great sanctity and potency.

The temple was also the 'House of the God'. Its design was similar to both the houses of the living and to the tombs, the houses of the dead. With human needs attributed to them, the gods needed food, drink, clothing, rest, and recreation; these were provided by means of rituals offered to the cult-statue. The

Right: A wooden plaque
showing Osiris, god
of the dead, and his
wife Isis
Opposite: A statue of
the god Horus in front
of his temple at Edfu

priests were literally the god's servants; their primary function
was to care for the god's statue and to perform the rituals. The
main purpose of the temple was thus regarded as mythological;
functional and, later, cosmological explanations were subsidiary.
Ritual and mythological requirements limited the architectural
forms of the Egyptian temple and ensured that the early forms
were repeatedly copied with few innovations. An element of
historical truth exists in the mythological version in terms of the
development of the temple. It originated as a simple reed shrine
which contained the cult-statue, in the pre-dynastic period
before 3100 BC. A forecourt, in which the god's ensign was
displayed, was set out in front of the shrine. Later stone-built
temples with their progression of forecourts and hypostyle halls

to the sanctuary at the rear of the building, still retained this basic layout.

Two distinct types of ritual existed. One was performed daily, in every temple, and was the same throughout Egypt; the other took place at regular intervals throughout the year and varied from temple to temple. The daily temple ritual was performed in every cult and mortuary temple; the priest visited the god's shrine, cleansed it, and dressed the statue in clean robes. It was presented with insignia, and finally with a morning meal. Food was presented again at noon and in the evening, when the statue was returned to its shrine for the night. In the mortuary temple this ritual was succeeded by another ritual in which food was offered to the previous kings of Egypt to ensure their acceptance of the present ruler, and to the living king's future dead, deified form. The unconsumed food was finally presented to the priests. The occasional rituals (the festivals) enacted some specific event in the cult of the god, such as the resurrection of Osiris at Abydos, or the sacred marriage between deities of neighbouring temples.

The walls of the temples, decorated with scenes carved in relief and originally painted in bright colours, provide a key to these rituals. The scenes, arranged in registers, are, in some parts of the temples, simply ceremonial or commemorative, but in the sacred areas, particularly in the sanctuary, they portray the sequence of rites once performed in that area of the temple. In these scenes the king is always shown performing the rite for the deity, thus supporting the fiction that the king alone performed the daily rituals in every temple in Egypt. In practice these sacred duties were carried out by the high priest of each temple, but in theory the king attended to the needs of the gods, since his unique relationship with them ensured their acceptance of the ritual and their bestowal, in return, of peace and prosperity for the king, his land, and subjects. Possibly the king performed the daily ritual in person in the great temple of the chief state god, as once the tribal chieftain of each area would have attended to the needs of his local deity. As mediator between gods and men the king presented food offerings to the gods, built their temples, and filled their treasuries with booty from wars and revenue from the state. In return, he received everlasting life and victory over his enemies. Thus was the prosperity and continuance of Egypt assured. The unique relationship between king and gods was believed to result from the fiction of his divine origin, resulting from the union between the great state god and the principal queen. As the divine heir he possessed the divine nature, but was regarded as the earthly incarnation of the god Horus and the son of Re, the

A typical wall relief from the temple of Dendera showing a ritual procession of royal figures making offerings

51

An amulet of Bes,
god of marriage and
merrymaking, worshipped
by ordinary people
in their homes

sun god. At death, each Horus-king became an Osiris, taking on
the eternal form of this god of the dead, and his Horus-title
passed to his successor.

Although the temple did not provide a centre of community
worship it played an important administrative, social, and
educational role in society. The temples were often wealthy
land-owners, possessing farms, vineyards, and mines; certain
revenues were also payable to them, and they employed a large
administrative staff to deal with these commitments. Extensive
storehouses attached to the temples housed the revenues paid in
kind. The administrators were permanent staff, as were the
cooks, butchers, gardeners, singers, musicians, and minor

clergy, who ensured the continuous organization of the temple. The priests, 'servants of the god', however, spent only a part of their lives at the temple. Usually hereditary, the priesthood was a secondary profession followed by certain upper-class families. The 'priests of Sekhmet' were also doctors, and some lawyers held the title 'priest of Ma'at'. Their time was divided between a secular occupation and religious duties, and they undertook three months of duty in a year at the temple. Certain taboos and customs regarding ritual cleanliness had to be observed during the period of temple duty, but otherwise they led normal lives, integrated into society, with careers, marriage, and families. In addition to religious duties, the priests also played an important educational role. There is some evidence to suggest that the temples provided centres of advanced learning, where priests instructed students in astronomy, the interpretation of dreams, geography, history, geometry, law, and medicine. In some instances the care of the sick may also have been carried out at the temples; in later times patients were accommodated in sanatoria attached to certain temples where they came in search of miraculous cures for physical and mental problems. The temple thus provided a focal point in Egyptian society and wielded considerable power.

Apart from the state cult there were the people's gods who listened to prayers and who could be called upon in time of need. Most popular were Bes, the dwarf god of love, marriage, and dancing, and Tauert, the goddess portrayed as a pregnant and upstanding hippopotamus, who protected women in child-birth. The large numbers of amulets and small statuettes in the form of these deities which are to be seen today in many museum collections, indicate the widespread worship of these deities by both rich and poor. Other popular deities, such as Astarte and Anat, were often of foreign origin, and Amun, the great state god of the New Kingdom, had an additional and rather surprising role as personal god of the necropolis workers at Thebes. But the deity with most influence, in both state and personal spheres, was Osiris. He was featured as a major character in the myths, and from the Middle Kingdom onwards was widely worshipped both in his capacity as a vegetation god and as the judge and god of the dead. Each king became an Osiris upon death, thus ensuring his resurrection as a ruler in the next world. Gradual democratization of funerary beliefs eventually enabled all worshippers of Osiris, whether rich or poor, to expect an individual hereafter. Credited in the later myths with the introduction of land-cultivation and the giving of laws, and always portrayed as a mummiform human king wearing a crown flanked by two feathers and carrying royal insignia, Osiris may

A bronze figurine of
the goddess Isis
nursing her son Horus.
She wears a typical
heavy wig surmounted by
the sun disc and horns

have originated as a human ruler of genius, perhaps murdered in
early quarrels. His great cult-centres were at Abydos and Busiris;
his annual festival held at Abydos commemorated his death and
re-enacted his resurrection as a ruler of the dead. Each
worshipper of Osiris was expected, if possible, to make at least
one pilgrimage to Abydos during his lifetime; model boats to
enable the deceased to make this journey were included as part
of the tomb equipment. Our main source for the myth of Osiris
is the Greek writer Plutarch. Although there are differing
versions, the basic story tells how Osiris was murdered by his
brother Seth (the embodiment of evil), and his body fragmented
and scattered throughout Egypt. Later, Isis, Osiris' sister and

54

A wooden statuette of Ptah-Sokar-Osiris, god of the underworld. Figures of this kind formed part of the funerary equipment in the Late Period and a papyrus was contained in the box on which it stands

widow, searched for the pieces in order to reunite them. She conceived posthumously the son of Osiris, the young god Horus. This Horus is to be distinguished from the falcon god, the original protector of royalty. Isis reared her son in the marshes, away from the wrath of Seth. When he was grown, Horus fought Seth to avenge his father's death. A bloody conflict ensued and finally a tribunal of gods sat in judgment and decided in favour of Horus, who was given the kingdom, while Osiris was resurrected as king and judge of the dead.

In addition to mummifying the body, the Egyptians spent lavishly on the tomb and its equipment. Apart from anthropoid coffins, brightly painted in many colours, and the sarcophagus

55

A Dynasty XII gold and enamelled pectoral from Riqqeh found round the neck of a mummy. When discovered, the corpse of an ancient tomb robber who had been in the act of removing the pectoral was in the collapsed tomb

which contained the body with its coffins, the deceased was provided with all the goods he had used and enjoyed in this life. Unlike the houses and palaces which were built of sun-dried brick, the tomb was constructed of stone since it was intended to endure forever. Much of the furniture and equipment which accompanied the dead is in a remarkable state of preservation, due to the hot, dry atmosphere of Egypt. This is our main source of information about the daily lives and habits of the ancient Egyptians. Materials from sites where the Egyptians actually lived still survives, but not in such quantities as from the tombs, and it is difficult not to reconstruct a somewhat one-sided view of their life, art, and religion. The only royal tomb which has been discovered virtually intact with its body and tomb goods is that of Tutankhamun in the Valley of the Kings at Thebes. This discovery in 1922 has since enabled a more precise and detailed study of funerary beliefs and customs to be made.

Apart from the objects which have been discovered in the tombs, scenes of funeral processions can also be seen in many non-royal tombs; these give some idea of the lavish preparations made for eternity. In addition to furniture (including chairs, beds, and caskets), fine linen clothing, sandals, and jewellery were included in the tomb equipment. Wealthy men and women both wore wigs when they went outside the house; these were made of either real hair or vegetable fibre and were worn over shaven heads or closely-cropped hairstyles. Heavy make-up was also used, partly as a protection against the sun, and both wigs and make-up were therefore stocked in the tomb for use in the after-life.

A series of amulets was inserted between the layers of wrappings round a mummy. Amulets were used in connection with burials in Egypt from the pre-dynastic period down to the Christian era, and were intended to protect the deceased from all the dangers which faced him in the future life. Best-known of the amulets is the scarab, a stone carved to represent a dung-beetle. This was believed to ensure resurrection and eternal life and generally to bring good luck; it was found not only among funerary equipment but also as a magical charm in rings and jewellery worn by the living.

In the Archaic Period (c. 3100-2686 BC) the burials of royalty and great nobles were sometimes surrounded by members of their families, retainers, and servants, who had been put to death and buried with their masters, either willingly or unwillingly, in order to serve the deceased in the next life. This custom soon ceased. Servant substitutes were provided either by figures in the reliefs on tomb walls or, during the First Intermediate Period and the Middle Kingdom, by wooden statuettes of brewers, bakers, sailors, and so forth, placed in the tomb. From the First Intermediate Period onwards these wooden models were replaced by *ushabti* figures. *Ushabtis* were small stone or wooden figures, *c.* 4-8 inches high. The name *Ushabti* is derived from the ancient Egyptian verb 'to answer'; it was believed that these figures would daily answer the call to forced labour on behalf of the dead person. Wealthy people often included one for each day of the year.

The so-called canopic jars also feature in funerary equipment. These stone jars, four in number, were used to contain the mummified viscera of the deceased; each jar was dedicated to one of the 'Four Sons of Horus'. Before the time of Dynasty XVIII the stoppers of the jars were all carved in the shape of human heads, but after this period only one deity, Imset, was shown human-headed; he tended the stomach and large intestines. The ape-headed jar, dedicated to Hapy, contained the small intestines, while the jackal-headed Duamutef was responsible for the lungs and heart; the hawk-headed Qebhsenuef looked after the liver and gall bladder. 'Canopic' is a term applied to these jars by early Egyptologists. They mistakenly connected them with the Greek legend of Canopus, the helmsman of Menelaus, who was buried at Canopus in the Delta and worshipped there in the form of a jar.

From what has been said it is clear that the Egyptians appear to have worshipped a multitude of gods, whose names, titles, and characteristics were frequently confusing, although each individual worshipper probably addressed his prayers only to his local god or group of deities. Every aspect of life was deeply rooted in religion; not only art and literature, but medicine, law, and education came under the direction of the gods. No clear distinction existed between the religious and secular life since the creation of the world and the establishment of kingship, law, ethics, and learning were thought to be the direct result of divine action. It was unnecessary to seek new solutions to religious or secular problems for it was believed that the gods had given mankind not only the physical world, but also a code of living which met every requirement of human existence. To a large extent this attitude explains the lack of desire for change which permeated society and which ensured its stability.

A typical faience *Ushabti* figure of Dynasty XXVI. It holds agricultural implements and is inscribed with a spell to enable it to perform manual labours for the deceased in the next world

3 Mummification

As WILL BE CLEAR ALREADY, the ancient Egyptians were deeply preoccupied with the after-life, and perhaps above all else with the need to preserve the body and likeness of the deceased. To this end they devised, after a great deal of trial and error, the process known today as mummification. The word 'mummy' is probably derived from the Persian word 'mummia' meaning bitumen. In certain areas of the world, including Persia, bitumen (or a bitumen-like substance) exudes naturally from the ground; the Persians believed that it had the power to cure certain physical ailments and prized it highly in consequence. Preserved bodies from ancient Egypt, particularly those of the Ptolemaic period (332-30 BC), often have a blackened appearance which was attributed, wrongly, to the process of soaking the body in bitumen. As a result, from the Ptolemaic period onwards the idea seems to have arisen that the embalmed bodies of the Egyptian dead would also provide a source of bituminous material which could be used in the preparation of medicines. Thus the Persian word mummia was applied to these embalmed bodies, and this has continued to the present-day, to give us the word mummy, so closely associated with ancient Egypt.

History of mummification

The earliest method of disposing of the dead, dating back to the pre-dynastic period (before 3100 BC) and for the poorer classes continuing throughout the dynastic period (3100-332 BC) was the burial of the naked body, perhaps covered by a reed or skin mat, in a shallow grave in the sand at the edge of the desert. Because agricultural land was so scarce and valuable the ancient Egyptians were unwilling to bury their dead near towns and villages. They chose instead to dispose of them in the immediately adjacent desert sands, and in doing so discovered, almost certainly accidentally, one way of preserving the body after death. The dryness of the desert sand and the hot rainless

The body of Asru, 'Chantress of Amun' at Karnak; showing the elaborately painted and inscribed coffin top with idealised features, and the well-preserved mummy, typical of the Late Period

58

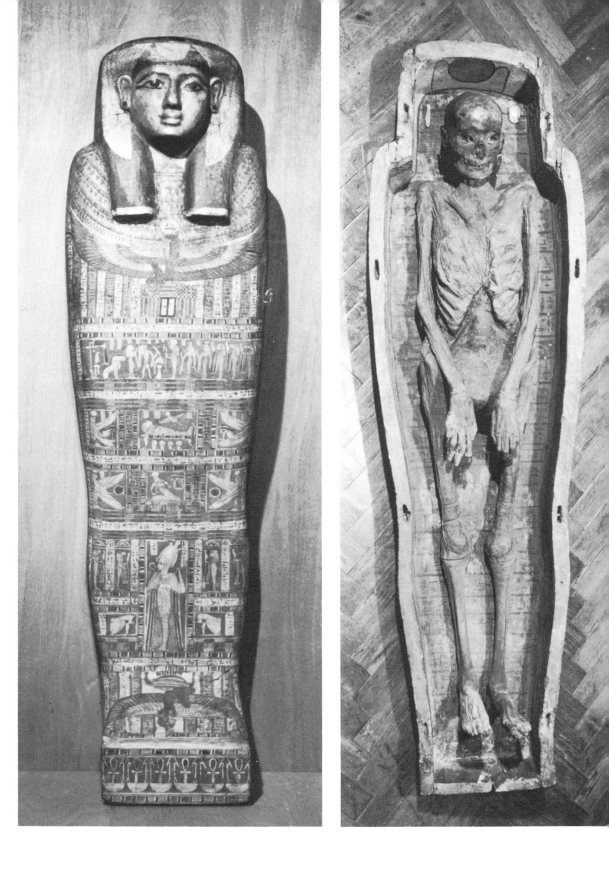

climate gradually dried out the corpse, the body fluids being absorbed into the sand. This process arrested decomposition quite quickly and while these conditions persisted the body could survive indefinitely. The idea that man's existence continued after death, requiring the preservation of the lifelike appearance of the body and a supply of food and drink, may have resulted from the accidental exposure of these long-dead and desiccated bodies, since the graves in which they were buried were often quite shallow, perhaps only two or three feet deep. These early examples cannot, strictly speaking, be classed as mummies, although with their skin and hair very often intact they are in a remarkable state of preservation.

With the development of increasingly sophisticated attitudes towards burial and the after-life, the royal family and the great nobles began to construct deeper and more elaborate tombs, as described in the last chapter, lined with wood or mud brick and often covered with a superstructure. The graves were filled with household goods and food, and the deceased was often enclosed in a wooden coffin. But this meant that the body was no longer in direct contact with the hot dry sand which had been the means of preserving pre-dynastic bodies, and the result was that decomposition became a serious problem. Religious beliefs about the after-life were by now, however, firmly established: the soul left the body at death but returned to it so that they could continue their existence together in the hereafter. It was essential, therefore, to preserve the body in as lifelike a condition as possible by some other means.

About fifty years ago Dr Quibell discovered an early attempt at mummification in the Dynasty II cemetery at Saqqara. A large mass of corroded linen was discovered between the outer bandages and the bones of a mummy, which possibly suggests that an attempt had been made to use crude natron as a preservative by applying it to the body's surface. Natron is a chemical which plays an important part in the process of mummification, as will emerge later. During the Archaic period (3100-2686 BC) and the early part of the Old Kingdom (2686-2181 BC), the loose body-cover was replaced by close-fitting linen bandages which emphasized the body contours. The limbs were wrapped separately; facial features, the breasts, and the genitalia were moulded in bandages impregnated with a gummy substance and details were added in paint. Underneath the bandages, however, the body continued to decompose. The end result was an elaborately wrapped and moulded skeleton, but a successful method of mummification had still to be found.

A mummy dating back to the Old Kingdom and probably to Dynasty V, was found at Meidum in 1891 by Sir Flinders Petrie and later presented to the Royal College of Surgeons. This showed that an attempt had been made to recreate the facial features and the organs with resin-soaked linen, while at the same time endeavouring to preserve the body tissues. A similar mummy was found near the Giza pyramids by the German scholar Junker. This was covered with linen and a layer of stucco plaster and attempted to portray the body features in detail. Earlier evidence of an attempt to prevent decomposition and to preserve the body tissues, rather than simply to create a modelled likeness on the body, dates back to Dynasty IV and the discovery of the canopic box of Queen Hetepheres, wife of Sneferu. This was found to contain viscera which had been removed from the body after death.

There is rather more evidence of mummification from the Middle Kingdom (1991-1786 BC) than from earlier periods. Generally, however, the preparation of the bodies was less painstaking and the results less successful. Although the viscera (lungs, liver, stomach, kidneys, etc.) were now regularly removed through an incision made in the left side and placed in canopic jars, less attention was given to preserving the body. Usually a thin coat of resin was applied to the skin surface and this left desiccation (the drying out of the body) incomplete so that decomposition soon set in. Although great care was lavished on the outward appearance of the mummies, inside there is usually only a jumble of bones with little or no evidence of soft tissue. The mummies of the Two Brothers in Manchester Museum, unwrapped by Dr Margaret Murray in 1906, belong to this period, and on these also there is little evidence of skin tissue. A group of royal bodies dating to Dynasty XI (immediately before the Middle Kingdom), discovered in the tombs below the temple of King Mentuhotep at Deir el-Bahari, provided an interesting exception to the practice current at the time, since there is no evidence that the viscera or the brain had been removed. The condition of the bodies is such that it suggests that either they were imperfectly treated with natron before wrapping or that no attempt at dehydration (the drying out of the body fluids) had been made.

In the New Kingdom (1552-1069 BC) two caches of royal mummies found at Thebes between 1881 and 1898 provide a great deal of information, although only about one class of society. Various methods of removing the brain were employed and the skull cavity was then packed with resin-soaked strips of linen. The positioning of the hands of the mummies varied according to sex and period. There were exceptions, but generally the mummies of women had their hands alongside their thighs, while mens' arms were fully extended, with the

A typical Egyptian Mummy and its casings

1a Body showing viscera which have been mummified, wrapped and returned to the body cavities
1b An alternative method of storing viscera, in Canopic jars
2 Mummy with incision in side of abdomen for removal of viscera; the incision has been sewn up
3a Mummy wrapped in bandages in the style of the New Kingdom. The crosses indicate the position of the most important amulets, inserted between the layers of bandaging
3b Mummy wrapped in bandages in the style common in the Graeco-Roman period

1b

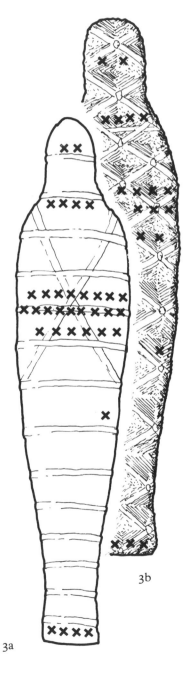

3b

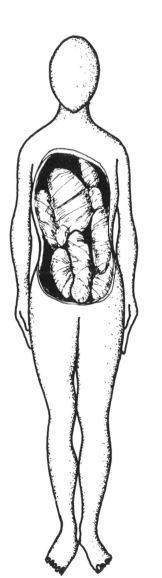

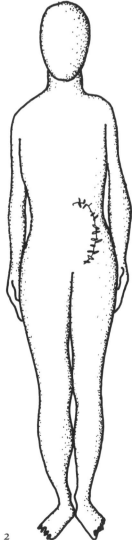

1a

2

3a

4 Cartonnage mask placed over the face and chest of
the wrapped mummy
5 The innermost anthropoid coffin in which the wrapped
mummy was placed
6 The outer rectangular wooden coffin which contained
the anthropoid coffin. This example, typical of the
Middle Kingdom style, shows the eyes on the side panel,
intended to enable the deceased to look out, and to
partake of the food and other offerings in the tomb
7 The stone chest or sarcophagus placed in the tomb.
This enclosed the wooden coffins and their contents.
The decorative inscriptions on the coffins and
the sarcophagus were magical texts to ensure the safe
passage of the deceased into the next world, and
a blessed existence in that world

4

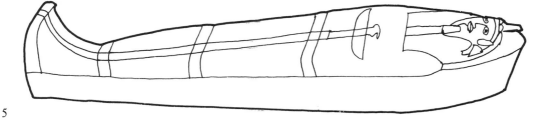

5

6

7

hands turned inwards at the side of the thighs. In the mummy of Tuthmosis II (1501-1491 BC), however, the arms were crossed over the breast, and this custom was adopted until Dynasty XXI when the arms were once again placed in the extended position. Nail-covers were attached to the fingers to ensure that the nails were not lost during the embalming process. The incision for the removal of the viscera was placed lower in the side of the mummy of Tuthmosis III (1490-1436 BC), another practice which continued until Dynasty XX. The mummy of the obese Pharaoh Amenophis III, who ruled towards the end of Dynasty XVIII, shows an attempt to restore the lifelike contours of the body by means of subcutaneous packing, a process which became widespread in Dynasty XXI. In Dynasty XIX an advance in embalming technique can be observed in the mummy of Ramesses II, which preserved the natural colouring of the skin, in contrast to the blackening and discolouration usually seen in earlier mummies.

Mummification was at its most skilful during Dynasty XXI. New techniques were developed which not only preserved the body and its appearance, but also attempted, often successfully, to reproduce the actual body contours and features of the person when alive. In earlier periods the embalmers had sought to reproduce a portrait likeness of the dead by applying material externally to the body surface. The method used in Dynasty XXI was to pack material under the skin surface. The viscera were removed through an incision in the left side, but were now packed into four separate parcels. The heart was left in the body. In each of the four parcels they placed a small figurine representing one of the four sons of Horus. Then the body cavity was filled up with the packages of viscera and other packing material. Several methods of removing the brain were practised, but the most common one was the forcing of an instrument up the nostril and through the intervening bone structure; the brain was then removed, perhaps using some type of ladle. The body cavity was packed through the wound in the left side and plugged with linen to prevent the escape of the packing materials, which included sawdust, butter, linen, and mud. The contours of the body were then restored by the introduction of packing under the skin through a series of small incisions made in its surface. The neck and cheeks were also packed, the face stuffing being introduced through the mouth.

Other means of identifying the mummy with the deceased included the insertion of artificial eyes into the eye sockets, the painting of the face, and often the whole body, with red ochre (for men) and yellow ochre (for women), and the supplementing of the natural hair with fake tresses. From the evidence available

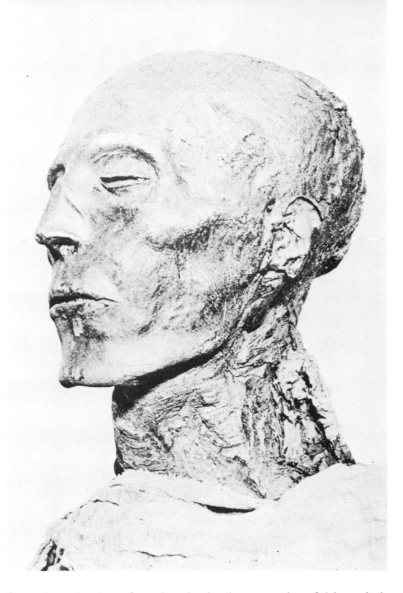

The mummy of the Dynasty XIX Pharaoh Seti I. This is perhaps the finest remaining example of the embalmer's skill

from the selection of royal and priestly mummies of this period, it seemed customary for male and female royal mummies to have their hands placed alongside their hips, while in the mummies of the priestly class, the hands were placed over the genital organs.

From Dynasty XXII onwards the standards of mummification gradually declined and more attention was paid to the exterior appearance of the mummy than to its internal preservation. By Dynasty XXVI the use of canopic jars was revived in place of the practice of returning the viscera to the body, or the parcels were simply placed between the legs. The decline in standards led also to the abandonment of subcutaneous packing – the method of packing beneath the skin to restore the original shape and contour of the body.

The heavily-resinated
outer wrappings and
coffin of the mummy
of Perenbast found
at Qurneh

In the Ptolemaic period (332-30 BC), with the progressive decline in religious beliefs, mummification became increasingly a commercial rather than a religious exercise. The outer wrappings were elaborate and outer bandages were often finely pleated into a series of geometrical patterns, interspersed with gilded studs. It was also customary to use three separate units of cartonnage: one piece to cover the head and shoulders; another, with representations of amulets, jewellery, and religious scenes,

over the chest; and a foot-piece painted to resemble a pair of sandals. Cartonnage (literally an outer covering) was made from waste-paper and sometimes included fragments of papyrus documents. Other mummies of this period display painted portrait heads on wooden panels which were placed over the face. Less attention was, however, paid to the body. The viscera were removed from some mummies and treated and returned to the body, while in others the body was either filled with balls of resin-soaked linen, broken pottery or mud, or it was filled with molten resin or bitumen which permeated the skin tissue and the bones. One of the main embalming agents of this period was resin. In molten form it was poured into the body cavity through the incision in the left side, and into the skull through the nostril after the removal of the brain. The molten resin frequently trapped maggots and beetles which were feeding off the decomposing bodies, thus killing them and preserving them between the bandages, to be rediscovered in modern times when the mummies were unwrapped. The eye-sockets and the mouth were filled with mud or linen. Mummies of this period have a blackened appearance, due to the use of molten resin over the skin surface.

There is considerable evidence to suggest that in the Ptolemaic period bodies were in an advanced state of decomposition when embalming was undertaken. The decaying body was obviously host to large numbers of insects before mummification, and x-ray evidence indicates that in some mummies the head had become detached from the body, or that limbs were missing, suggesting that the body had fallen apart during embalming. This could be due to several factors, including the fall in standards of craftsmanship and delay in dealing with cheaper burials because of pressure of work. However, according to ancient sources, the bodies of certain women (those who had been beautiful, or had been the wives of eminent men) were not handed over to the embalmers until three or four days after death, when decomposition would have begun, presumably to inhibit necrophilia.

During the Roman period (30 BC–AD 641) mummification deteriorated still further. A thick coating of resinous substances was applied to the body, so that it is not usually possible to tell if the viscera have been removed or not. The outer wrapping became increasingly elaborate and gilded head and chest covers, often inlaid with imitation jewellery, were frequently incorporated in the mummy. Later in the Roman period, during the Christian era, the elaborate outer wrappings continued to be used, but the treatment of the body was now superficial. The religious beliefs no longer required that the likeness of the deceased should be preserved, and with the Mohammedan invasion of Egypt, in AD 641, mummification finally ceased.

ANCIENT SOURCES Apart from the evidence provided by the mummified remains, the only ancient account of the process used in the preservation of the dead that has come down to us is not from an Egyptian source, but from the works of two Greek authors who wrote about Egypt: Herodotus in the fifth century

A typical mummy case of the Graeco-Roman period showing a young man holding a bunch of flowers. The portrait panel over the face (above) would have been painted during the lifetime of the deceased, displayed in his house, and cut to size and incorporated in the funerary wrappings as part of the mummification procedure

BC, and Diodorus Siculus about 400 years later. Egyptian texts, and the writings of other classical authors in which embalming is mentioned, make only passing reference to this process and do not consider the techniques used by the embalmers. We must therefore rely on the writings of Herodotus, who doubtless received all his information from the priests and who wrote in a relatively late period when, as we have seen, the process was gradually dying out. His account differs only in detail from that of Diodorus Siculus.

According to Herodotus, the body of the deceased was brought to the embalmers and wooden models were shown to the relatives who, according to their means, selected one of the three available methods of embalming. The cheapest method, used to prepare the bodies of the poor, was simply to rinse the body through with a purge, to preserve it for seventy days, and then to return it to the family. The second method was to fill the belly of the corpse with cedar oil by means of a syringe, the body being plugged to prevent the oil escaping. After an appointed number of days the cedar oil was released from the body, bringing with it the liquified organs and bowels; the body was then returned to the family. The third and most expensive method was inevitably the most elaborate. The brain was drawn out through the nose, partly with a hooked iron and partly by the use of medicines which liquified the brain. An incision was made with 'a sharp Ethiopian knife' in the side of the abdomen and the viscera were removed, except for the heart (believed to be the seat of the emotions) and the kidneys. The viscera were cleaned with palm wine mixed with various spices, and treated with natron. They were then placed either in canopic jars or packed in bandages and replaced in the body cavity. The body was cleansed and rinsed through with palm wine and crushed incense; it was then filled with crushed myrrh, cassia, and other spices and sewn up again. It was then preserved by means of natron, although there is some controversy over the method actually employed. It was originally thought that the bodies were actually immersed and soaked in baths of natron but it is also possible that dry natron was used. This is discussed later in the chapter. The preservation process continued for not longer than seventy days. Then the body was washed again and wrapped in strips of fine linen cloth which had been coated with gum. Amulets were inserted between the wrappings, the relevant religious practices were observed, and then the body was returned to the family in its wooden coffin.

It has to be emphasized that Herodotus was writing in the fifth century BC, when the major periods of Egyptian history (the Old, Middle, and New Kingdoms) were long since gone.

However accurate his account was for the fifth century, it was not necessarily true for the earlier periods, including those when mummification was at its most efficient. Techniques must have varied from period to period, even if the basic principles remained the same, i.e., the removal of the viscera and the dehydration or drying out of the body by means of natron, thus arresting the process of decompostion.

EXPERIMENTAL MUMMIFICATION   As part of the overall research programme, which is described in detail in the second part, one member of the team, Mr R. Garner of Manchester Museum, carried out a series of experiments designed to test the basic processes of mummification, particularly the method mentioned by Herodotus as the most costly and therefore likely to have been reserved for the upper classes.

Natron, the main chemical agent in mummification, is a salt mixture occurring in natural deposits. Samples from modern deposits show a large proportion of sodium carbonate and sodium bicarbonate, more commonly known as washing soda and baking soda respectively. These salts form the natron proper and they act, as far as mummification is concerned, by desiccating or drying out the body tissues. Also present, but as impurities, are sodium chloride and sodium sulphate (common salt and Glauber's salt). However, ancient, as opposed to modern, samples of natron tend to contain rather less of the true natron salts (sodium carbonate and sodium bicarbonate), and this may be explained by their susceptibility to decompostion. If the samples had been used in mummification then these salts would have been affected, and open exposure to atmospheric influences over a period of a thousand years or more could also be expected to have had some effect.

For experimental purposes 'artificial' natron mixtures were made up, reflecting the variations in naturally occurring deposits. Rats and mice were chosen as subjects because of their availability and convenient size. In early experiments they were shaved, but parallel tests indicated that the fur had little significant influence and the shaving was in consequence discontinued. The body of the animal was opened, the organs removed, the body cavity packed with natron and then closed with a few stitches. The body was then laid on a thick bed of natron salt and covered to a similar depth with additional salt. The organs were also buried in the natron salt. During the first series of experiments the animals were removed from the natron at various intervals in order to determine the minimum period necessary to render the body stable and no longer susceptible to decay. On removal from the natron the excess was brushed from

A sequence of photographs
taken during Roy Garner's
experiments in mummi-
fication techniques.
After a series of tests
using liquid and dry
methods he discovered
that the latter produced
the best results.
(1) A rat before
dissection; (2) opening
its body cavity;

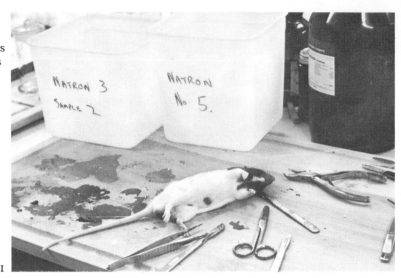

1

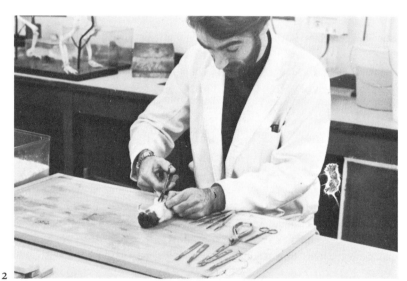

2

3

(3) packing with dry
natron; (4) stitching
after packing;
(5 and 6) burying
the corpse in dry
natron where it was left
for about thirty to
forty days

4

5

6

the body and the body cavity was emptied. The animal was then left exposed to the atmosphere and any signs of continuing decay were noted.

It has long been assumed that the natron employed in mummification was used as a solution in water rather than in its solid state. However, recent re-examination of the evidence has indicated that this is unlikely to be the case. The misunderstanding probably arose from a mistranslation of Herodotus' original Greek, and also from incorrect interpretation of the evidence from the mummies themselves. The new theory, that the natron was used in its solid state, has received support from experiments involving the mummification of birds, and in order to substantiate the evidence further a second series of experiments was carried out. Natron solutions of various strengths were made up and the eviscerated animals were totally immersed in them. It soon became clear that natron in solution was unlikely to have been the method used by the Egyptians for preserving their dead. All the animals treated in this manner showed evidence of considerable decomposition. The most obvious was the strong smell of putrefaction which became noticeable after a few days and which persisted until the animals had completely dried out. The degree of decay, and its effects, varied according to the composition of the natron solution and the length of time the animals were immersed. However, in all cases they were almost impossible to handle when they were taken from the solution. Some had lost large patches of fur and many were discoloured and distended. The body tissue tended to be very soft, often being of a pulpy or jelly-like consistency, and anything but the most careful handling caused the skin and underlying muscle to become detached from each other.

In contrast, the animals treated with dry natron were usually odour-free, firm, and easy to handle. Various compositions of natron produced quite distinct differences, both in the condition of the body and in the state of the natron from which it had been removed. Where high proportions (60 per cent or more) of sodium carbonate and sodium bicarbonate (the true natron salts), were present, the body tended to be fairly dry and rigid. In the natron itself, most of the soiling was confined to the layer immediately around the body, leaving the rest of the chemical fairly dry and fresh. However, the presence of 40 per cent or more of sodium chloride (common salt) in the natron mixture tended to leave the body in a more flexible state; in this case the soiling extended for quite some distance from the body. Reuse of the natron progressively reduced its effectiveness, the result of which is most easily seen as an increase in the time required for the body to be rendered stable. This leads to a greater degree of decay before desiccation takes place, in which case the odour of putrefaction becomes more noticeable. Due to the greater amount of soiling, natron samples with a high proportion of sodium chloride (common salt) degraded more rapidly than those containing a lower level of impurities.

Investigation of the two other, less expensive, methods of mummification mentioned by Herodotus was carried out by injecting the body with either oil (of various kinds) or water. The animals were then buried in dry natron as in the first series of experiments. These animals gave off a moderate odour during treatment. Those treated with water showed considerable signs of decay, and fur and skin were easily displaced when they were handled. The animals injected with oil were noticeably less affected. When the natron treatment was complete any remaining fluid was removed and the animals were allowed to dry out. During this period they showed considerable distortion and shrinkage.

Animals treated with dry natron alone appeared to reach a stable condition in thirty to forty days, longer times being required if high proportions of impurities were present, or if the natron had been reused. This figure of thirty to forty days appeared to be fairly constant regardless of the size of the animal, provided that the amount of natron used was high in relation to the size of the body. Injected animals, on the other hand (i.e., injected with oil or water), showed little sign of drying in this time, and some of them were found to have retained considerable fluid after eighty days.

The period of thirty to forty days may well indeed be the duration of the treatment with natron which the Egyptians used for their dead. Less time would not have produced satisfactory preservation and longer periods would appear to have been unnecessary. The remainder of the seventy days mentioned by Herodotus as the total period of mummification could well have been occupied by other processes: anointing with oils, wrapping, and religious rituals.

The final condition of the body after mummification was influenced by several factors. Too little natron packed in and around the body would either allow decay to reach an advanced state before it really began to dry or would make proper desiccation impossible. Frequent use of the same supply of natron would reduce its effectiveness, producing similar consequences. Finally, variations in the composition of the natron itself (i.e., in the percentage of impurities) would have their own effects, and may well have influenced the other two factors as well. Many cases of badly preserved mummies may be attributed to these causes, although the condition of the body before mummification, and its subsequent treatment, must also be considered.

However, these factors alone seem unlikely to account for the poor state of preservation seen in so many late Egyptian mummies. Such consistently bad examples of the embalmer's work are, perhaps, more likely to be due to a lowering of professional standards. As a result of changing social and religious attitudes more attention was paid to the artificial adornment of the mummy than to the initial preparation of the body, leading to a gradual but inevitable decline in the embalmer's art. Less-skilled embalmers would have been employed, further hastening the decline of the craft. This could easily have resulted in such shortcomings as the use of too little natron, too frequent use of the same supply, and possibly even the failure to treat the body for the required length of time. These could only result in the return of very poorly preserved bodies to the relatives, a state of affairs which would further reduce demand for the traditional, high art of the embalmer.

Mummies in Manchester Museum

The collection of Egyptian antiquities in Manchester Museum is among the finest and most comprehensive in this country. Many are from sites excavated by the great Egyptologist, Sir Flinders Petrie, and were added to the museum collection through the generous financial support given to several of Petrie's excavations by Dr Jesse Hawarth, a Manchester businessman. The museum buildings, which house not only the Egyptology galleries but also the other collections in which the museum specializes, were also established through the financial contributions of Jesse Hawarth and other donors.

A fair selection of the different types of mummification from the various periods of Egyptian history is provided by the seventeen human and twenty-two animal mummies in the museum. Since the human mummies form the basis of the research carried out as part of the Manchester Museum Mummy Project a few biographical details may help to place them in context. The mummies are referred to by the accession numbers given to them when they became part of the museum collection, and are dealt with period by period, starting with the Middle Kingdom, the earliest period represented in the Manchester collection.

THE MIDDLE KINGDOM (1991-1786 BC; NOS 21470, 21471) The oldest mummies in the Museum collection date to around 1900 BC and are known as 'the Two Brothers'. They were unwrapped in 1906 by the Museum's first curator of Egyptology, Dr Margaret Murray, and examined by her small team of scientists and medical specialists. The complete tomb-group came to the museum from Rifeh, a site in Middle Egypt, and includes an elaborately painted anthropoid (i.e., body-shaped) coffin and an outer coffin for each brother, in addition to two model boats to travel upstream and downstream after death, wooden models of servants, and statuettes of the brothers. The coffin inscriptions inform us that the mummies were both 'son(s) of Aa-Khnum', but they were possibly children of different husbands and therefore half-brothers. Nekht Ankh was probably of the non-negroid type, and was possibly a eunuch, while there is some indication that Khnum Nakht had negroid features. Nekht Ankh was probably about sixty years of age at death and, according to custom, his viscera were removed from his body, mummified, and placed in a set of four canopic jars. The mummy of Khnum Nakht, who probably died in early middle age, is less well-preserved, and has no accompanying set of canopic jars.

THE NEW KINGDOM (1552-1069 BC; NOS 3496 and 9354) The only example of a poor person's burial in the museum collection is the child mummy wrapped in a reed mat tied with ropes at either end. This comes from Gurob, a New Kingdom town site, and dates to Dynasty XVIII. The second mummy is that of Khary, a priest of Amun, and dates to Dynasty XIX. It was brought to England in its decorated coffin in 1893, when it was said to be the oldest passenger transported to Manchester arriving via the Ship Canal.

The reed coffin containing a baby. A gruesome detail is the toes sticking out at one end

THIRD INTERMEDIATE PERIOD (1069-525 BC; NOS 10881, 1976.51A, 1777 AND 5053) Four female mummies date to this period, the first two being good examples from Dynasty XXI, while the others are from Dynasty XXV. The mummy of Ta-ath probably came from Luxor. It was brought to England by Mr John Frewen of Brickwell House, near Rye, Sussex. Suspected of bringing bad luck to the family, the mummy was placed on loan in Hastings Museum in 1926, and was finally transferred to Manchester Museum in 1948. The mummy still has its original painted wooden coffin and was partly unwrapped years ago.

The second mummy was given to the museum in 1975 by Professor W. E. Kershaw, a member of the Manchester Mummy team. It still has its original painted wooden coffin and the body is well-preserved, with the embalmer's incision in the left side of the abdomen clearly visible.

Mummy No 1777, complete with two decorated wooden coffins, had already been unwrapped when it arrived in the museum in 1825, the first Egyptian accession of any importance. Named Asru, and entitled 'Chantress of Amun', the mummy probably came from Luxor.

The last mummy in this group is bandaged and covered with a thin coat of resin which fixes it firmly to the coffin; this is also covered with resin and decorated with designs painted in yellow. Lotus flowers, still preserved, rest on top of the mummy. Named Perenbast, and also entitled 'Chantress of Amun', this mummy was found, together with that of a man, in a previously unopened courtyard tomb at Qurneh.

THE GRAECO-ROMAN PERIOD (332 BC-AD 641; NOS 1769, 2109, 9319, 1768, 1767, 1775, 20638, 1766 AND 1770) Three mummies in this group are of children. One, that of a girl, was discovered with the mummies of a woman and two other children at Hawara. The upper part of the body is covered with a gilded cartonnage with inlaid eyes. Jewellery is also indicated on the cartonnage which is set with imitation stones. A canvas wrapper, painted with scenes of deities gilded on to a pink background, encases the lower part of the mummy, which probably dates to about AD 135. The two other child mummies from Hawara provide examples of the bandagers' skill during this period; the lower parts of both mummies have elaborate diagonal bandaging, interspersed with gilt studs. Mummy No 2109 has a cartonnage head-cover with a gilded face, and Mummy No 9319 was originally covered with a portrait panel which is in Cairo Museum.

From the same period and site there are three male adult mummies. One is of a young man, with diagonal bandaging covering the lower part and a fine portrait panel over the face, in which he is shown wearing a laurel wreath. The second adult also has a portrait panel over the face, showing the deceased as a bearded, older man; the upper part of the body is covered in stucco and painted, while the lower part is encased in canvas decorated with painted figures or deities on a red background. The third mummy is covered with painted red stucco which has been brightly glazed with gum or resin; on this background gilded figures of deities are modelled in low relief. Over the face there is one of the earliest portrait panels, showing the deceased as an elderly man; his name is given in an inscription across the chest as 'Artemidorus'. The mummy was discovered in a brick-lined chamber, together with another Artemidorus (now in the British Museum), and a lady, Thermoutharin (now in Cairo Museum).

The three remaining mummies in the group are female. Two of them are from the Fayum, the great depression to the west of the Nile. One, named 'Demetria, wife of Icaious', has a gilded cartonnage head and breast-cover, set with imitation stones representing jewellery, and inlaid eyes; the lower part of the mummy is covered in canvas decorated with four rows of deities on a red background. The second female also has a gilded cartonnage head and breast-cover, again inlaid with imitation stones, and representing the woman holding a bunch of red flowers.

The third mummy was the one unwrapped and investigated in 1975 by the Manchester team, No 1770. The outer wrappings were of a dull brown colour, and the general appearance of the mummy was unimpressive, but it did possess a rather fine cartonnage head-piece with inlaid eyes and eyebrows. A cartonnage breast-cover, gilded nipple-covers, gilded finger and toe-covers, and ceremonial sandals, were discovered within the wrappings, in addition to the imitation legs and feet which were added to replace the missing lower limbs and thus ensure the completeness of the person's body in the after-life. This mummy came to Manchester Museum in 1896 from a private collection, and although it may also have come from the excavations at Hawara, there is no record of exactly where it was found. The sex of the person is uncertain and our investigations showed that the men who wrapped the body in the Ptolemaic period were probably also not sure whether they were preparing a man or a woman for the after-life.

The mummies in Manchester Museum, therefore, range in date from Dynasty XII to the period of Roman rule in Egypt, a time-span of some 2,000 years. Of these, four came from the excavations of Sir Flinders Petrie in the Fayum and were given

The mummy of an elderly
man, Artemidorus,
which has one of the
earliest examples of
a portrait panel

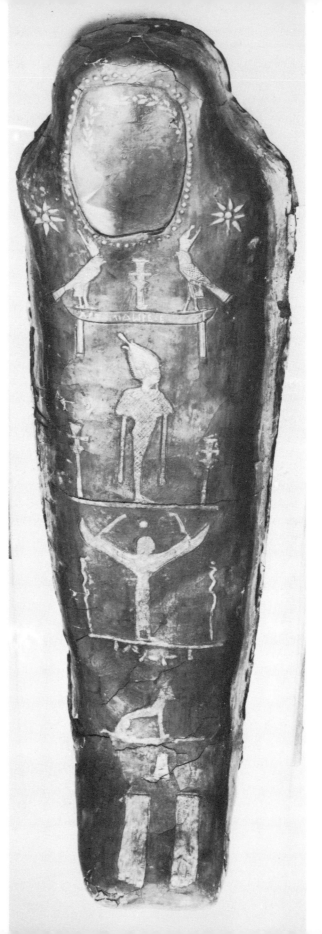

to the museum by Dr Jesse Hawarth; others came through the British School of Archaeology in Egypt and the Egyptian Research Account. One mummy was donated by the Committee of Ancoats Art Museum in Manchester, and another came to the museum from the Frewen family, via Hastings Museum. Two mummies were received from the collection of M. E. Robinow and three other mummies came from individual donors.

Mummies have had a fascination for the western world for many centuries. 'Unrollings' of mummies were performed before specially invited audiences, and Thomas Pettigrew, a London surgeon, made a living in the middle of the nineteenth century by carrying out dissections. As we have seen, 'mummy' (i.e., a piece of a mummified body) was also used in medicine. The earliest use is attributed to a Jewish physician of Alexandria, about AD 1200, but mummy continued to be incorporated in medicines throughout western Europe for several centuries, and is attested in the writers of the seventeenth and eighteenth centuries.

However, mummification made a much greater contribution to the development of medical science in ancient Egypt. Observations made during the process of mummification encouraged the early Egyptians to become aware of the anatomy of the human body, and unlike the beliefs of some other ancient societies, the opening of the body after death was not considered to be a violation of the deceased. Knowledge of the body, gained through the techniques of mummification, enabled the Egyptians to establish the beginnings of medical science. This encouraged foreign scholars, including Greeks, to visit Egypt to study these skills.

Now the situation is reversed: the techniques of modern science and medicine can be used to examine ancient mummified remains and to provide us with information regarding the diseases, causes of death, living conditions, and funerary beliefs of the ancient Egyptians.

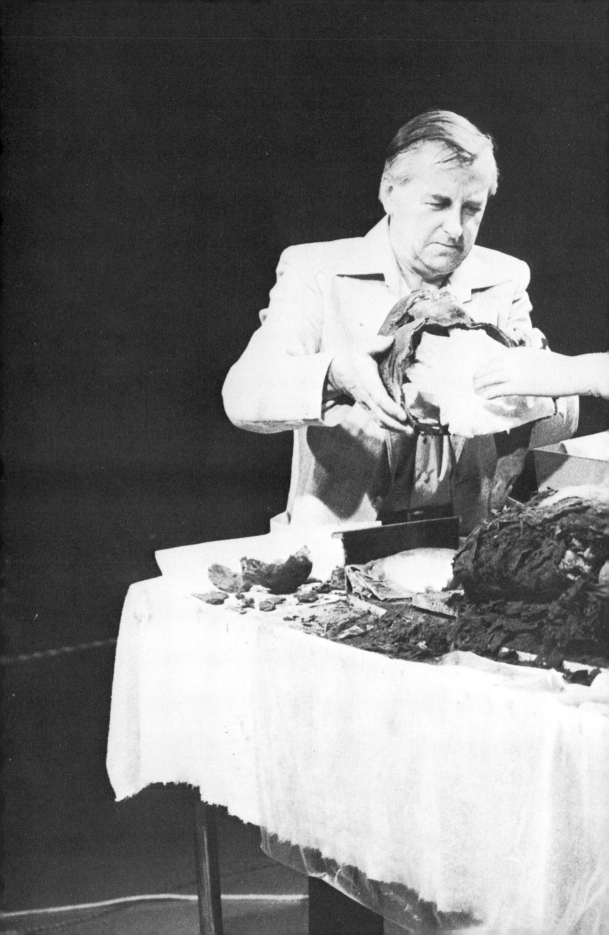

Part II

THE INVESTIGATION

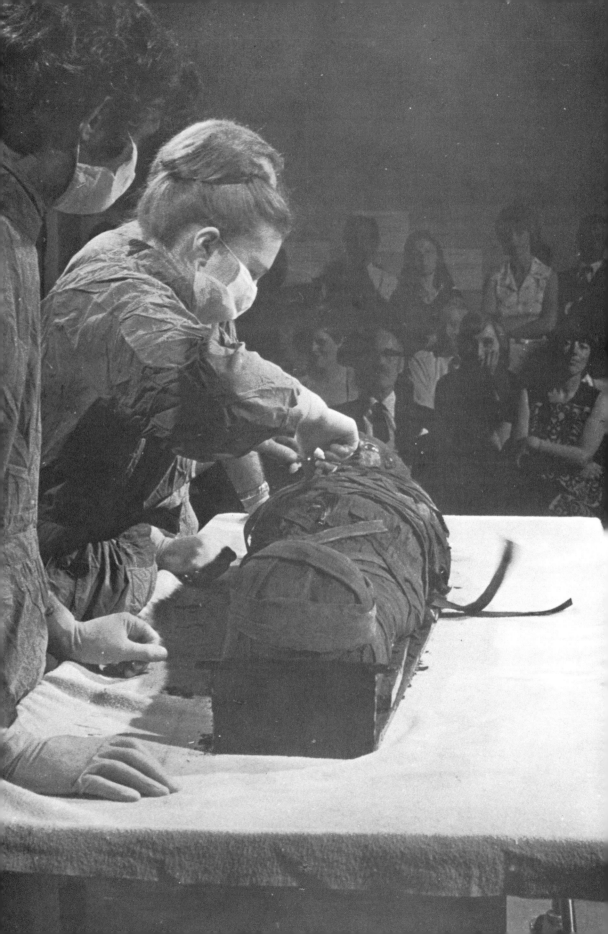

4 The Unwrapping

THE MUMMY TEAM Apart from Dr Rosalie David, Egyptologist at the Manchester Museum, the earliest members of the team included Dr D. M. Dixon, Lecturer in Egyptology and Curator of the Flinders Petrie Museum at University College, London, and Mr F. F. Leek, a dental surgeon with considerable previous experience in the study of the teeth of mummies, including those of Tutankhamun. Mr R. A. H. Neave, Assistant Director of the Department of Medical Illustration at Manchester Royal Infirmary, agreed to try to reconstruct the heads and facial appearance of some of the mummies, starting with the skull bone, and as will be seen, he had considerable success. Mr R. Garner, a member of Manchester Museum conservation staff, investigated the mummification process, carrying out some interesting experiments on animals which have been described in Chapter III.

They were joined by the two medical members of the team: Dr I. Isherwood, now Professor of Diagnostic Radiology at the University of Manchester, was to do a complete radiological survey of the mummies, with the assistance of Superintendent Radiographer Miss H. Jarvis; while Dr E. Tapp, now consultant histo-pathologist at the group laboratory, Preston Royal Infirmary, was brought in to perform an autopsy on mummy 1770 and to carry out an histo-pathological examination of the tissues of this and the other mummies. Dr Tapp also did some electron-microscopy of the mummified tissue and collaborated in this with Dr A. Curry, a zoologist and electron-microscopist at the University Hospital of South Manchester. In addition, Dr Curry undertook a study of the insects and other small invertebrate animals found within the mummies and their wrappings. Another member of the team was Dr F. Leach, Director of the Drug Identification Centre of St Mary's Hospital, Manchester. His interests included the examination of the wrappings of the mummy and the identification of the resins which were used in the mummification process. Many others took part in the

Previous pages:
The cartonnage mask is removed from mummy 1770 for conservation

Opposite: Work begins on cutting the outer cross-bandages in front of an invited audience

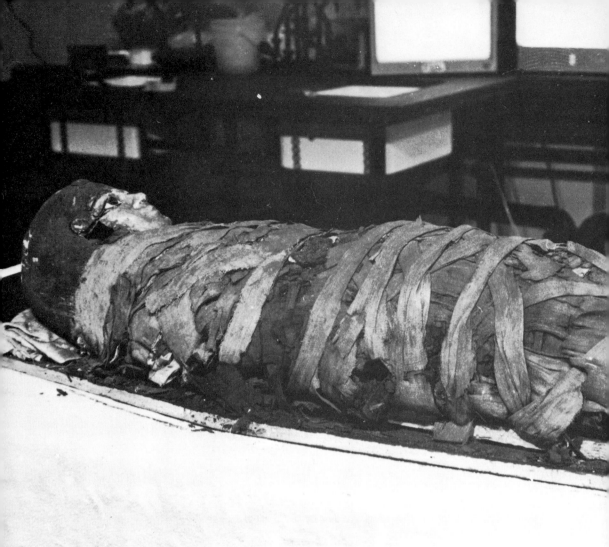

investigation, including Professor W. E. Kershaw, who contributed a mummy to the Manchester Museum collection, and Dr A. Ahmed, who hoped to find some breast tissue in the mummies. Later the team was joined by Chief Detective Inspector A. Fletcher of the Greater Manchester Police, who took fingerprints of the mummies, and by Dr G. W. A. Newton of the Department of Chemistry at the University of Manchester, who carried out Carbon-14 dating determinations on mummy 1770. Several of these team members were enthusiastically assisted in their research by their co-workers.

THE PREPARATION With the team assembled the next task was to persuade the Museum authorities to allow the unwrapping of a mummy. There is still a good deal of disagreement amongst Egyptologists about its desirability. The arguments against unwrapping had to be considered seriously, for there is obviously a limited number of mummies and the number is depleted each time one is unwrapped. Moreover, the trustees of many museums do not have the authority to allow the destruction of any specimens in their care which are irreplaceable. In addition, since the bodies were originally mummified to preserve them for the after-life, religious aspects must be considered, and it might be regarded by some as an act of desecration to unwrap and dismember a body preserved for this reason. While the team were fully aware of these views, it was felt that since Dr Murray's investigations had taken place seventy years ago, the amount of new information to be gathered from the techniques which could be applied today to the study of an unwrapped mummy outweighed other considerations. Fortunately the Museum authorities agreed and permission to proceed with the unwrapping was given.

The next task was to choose a suitable mummy. Clearly one with decorative bandaging, suitable for display purposes in the Museum, could not be used. By the same token, mummies of which the exact provenance or find spot was known had to be excluded. A mummy with something of a mystery surrounding it would clearly be a very suitable choice and by a stroke of luck one was available, a mummy which could be referred to only by its museum number, 1770. X-rays taken some years ago had indicated that the mummy was that of a child aged about thirteen years. Curiously, the x-rays also showed that the lower parts of the legs were missing. Little was known of the source of the mummy, but it had come into the possession of the museum in about 1896. Sir Flinders Petrie's diary, and a letter he sent to a friend after a visit to Manchester Museum, indicate that No 1770 possibly came from his excavations at Hawara in Egypt. The exact date of the mummy was not known, but it was thought to be from the Graeco-Roman period of Egyptian history.

In addition to the mystery of how the legs had been amputated, the nature of a rounded object close to the ends of the leg bones in the original x-rays gave rise to a good deal of speculation. It bore some resemblance to the head of a human foetus and so suggested the possibility of a newly-born child being included in the wrappings of a mother dying soon after giving birth. On the other hand, was there something more sinister here? At the time, unmarried Egyptian girls who became pregnant might well have suffered mutilation or even been stoned to death, and clearly the amputations could have been the result of such an ordeal. Such speculation was based on only flimsy evidence but it certainly added interest to the unwrapping of the anonymous 1770.

Mummy 1770 awaits dissection. Its fine cartonnage mask provides a stark contrast to the disarray of the outer wrappings

A suitable room had to be found for the unwrapping, one large enough to give the team an adequate amount of space in which to work and one which would accommodate the large numbers of people who were involved in the project. It soon became apparent that the number of visitors would have to be controlled but space still had to be found for the press and television cameras, for the unwrapping of the mummy was rapidly becoming newsworthy. Moreover, in view of the uniqueness of the occasion, it was considered important to have a complete record on film of the unwrapping, including both ciné-film and still photographs.

Instruments for the unwrapping and autopsy were selected, bearing in mind that no one knew what condition the body would be in once the bandages had been removed. Electric saws and stainless steel chisels of the type used in modern autopsies were included in case the tissues were impregnated with resins, some of which leave them rock-hard. Preparations were also made for the careful recording of the position of the bandages and the documentation of any tissues removed at the autopsy.

As the day for the unwrapping finally approached mummy 1770 had to be transported from the Museum, first to the Department of Radiology at Manchester Royal Infirmary, where Professor Isherwood and Miss Jarvis were to do a complete radiological survey of the mummy, using the sophisticated equipment to be described later. The journey from the Museum to the Infirmary was completed safely, and a few days later the mummy was moved again, this time to the University Medical School where the unwrapping was at last to take place.

THE UNWRAPPING All the preparations being complete, it was an expectant team which gathered under the glare of the arc lights, before a large audience, for the start of the unwrapping on 10 June 1975. After Mr Paul Jordan of BBC Television had explained how his cameras would be positioned, Dr Rosalie David and Dr Tapp discussed the best way to start the unwrapping. The outer layers of bandages, about four inches wide, were arranged in either a circular or diagonal pattern. When these had been removed much wider pieces of material running lengthways were revealed. Dead insects found among the wrappings were carefully removed for study. As the lengthwise bandages were removed the lower part of the cartonnage mask was exposed. After cleaning, this proved to be an excellent example of its type, with delicately executed designs painted on it. The part of the mask covering the neck and right side of the face was found to be damaged, the head being completely separated from the lower part. When the

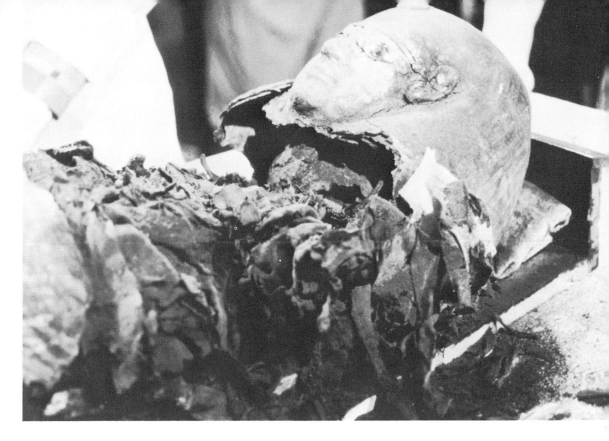

damaged part of the mask had been removed it was found that the bones of the neck and skull were fragmented and could be removed piecemeal. The bones forming the upper jaw and face were intact and after cleaning damage to the left side of the nose was revealed, where the embalmers had introduced the iron hook during the removal of the brain. A similar defect was seen in the base of the skull where the hook had emerged in the cranial cavity. A further interesting feature noted at the time was the presence of red and blue paint on the surface of the cranial bones. The cartonnage mask was removed and preserved.

Removal of more bandages now revealed the arms crossed in front of the chest. There was very little flesh remaining on them or in the chest wall and what there was proved to be extremely dry and friable. When the hands came into view gold finger-stalls were seen. Further gold leaf was found loose amongst the wrappings, together with two gold nipple-covers. Removal of the remaining bandages from the trunk showed that the thoracic cavity was completely empty. At this time the peculiar distribution of the resin in the intravertebral discs was seen. Similar resin was observed at the ends of the long bones. The abdomen and pelvis were packed with bandages and mud, the bones of the pelvis being broken. A careful search of the packing failed to show any signs of the organs which normally

Some of the most complete funerary equipment of 1770 were the cartonnage head and chest covers. The top photograph shows the damage to the part of the mask covering the neck. The lower shows the brightly-coloured breast cover which can be seen in greater detail on page 95

89

Above right: When the outer wrappings had been removed the arms could be seen to be folded across the chest, in imitation of the god Osiris.
Right: Gold nail-covers were found in position on some of the fingers and others lay in the surrounding bandages

occupy the abdomen and pelvis. However, a hard mass, one inch in diameter, was found in the abdominal wall, in a position corresponding with that of a small opaque object seen by Professor Isherwood on his radiographs. This proved to be the calcified remains of a parasite, Guinea-worm, and will be described in detail later. A second interesting discovery made at this time was a small roll of bandages which lay outside the pelvic cavity and was continuous with the bandages covering the front of the abdomen. There is little doubt that this was an artificial phallus.

The unwrapping of the legs then began and a further exciting find was made when the bandages were removed from the 'feet'. These proved to be artificial. The right foot was an intricate

Below left: A view of the amputated legs showing that the right one had been artificially lengthened. Both had been fitted with false feet.
Below: the decorated sandals which had been placed over the false feet

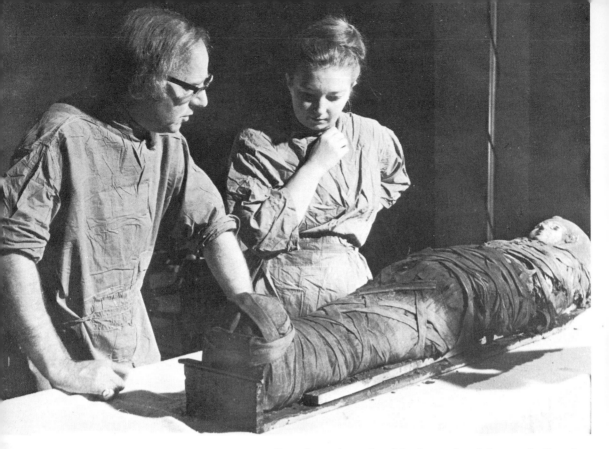

Above: Drs David and
Tapp discuss methods
of unwrapping 1770

Opposite above: Dr David
making the first cuts
in the outer wrapping
which exposed the
cartonnage cover whose
existence was hitherto
unrevealed

Opposite below: a detail
of the highly-coloured
cartonnage chest cover
with its painted scenes
of resurrection

Overleaf: Mummy 1770
after the outer
wrappings over the chest
cover had been removed

structure of reeds and mud, with the ends of the reeds forming
the toes; the left 'foot' consisted merely of an irregular mass of
mud and reeds. Gilded toe-nail covers, similar to those found on
the fingers were provided for the 'feet'; and beautifully decorated
slippers had been placed over the soles. The legs had been
amputated, the left below the knee, through the tibia, and the
right above the knee, through the femur. The right leg, however, had been lengthened by an artificial leg of wood covered
with mud to make it the same length as the left. Removal of the
mud from the end of the femur showed pieces of wood splinting
the bone to the artificial limb. It was obvious that the bandages
were so closely applied to the bone that very little, if any, flesh
could have been attached to it when the bandages were applied.
The illustrations also show the irregular amputation line and
the fact that there is no bony callus on the ends of the femur.

CONCLUSIONS These observations give rise to certain deduc-
tions – and much speculation. The body was poorly preserved,
very little recognizable skin, muscle, or soft tissue being present.
Such tissue as was detected proved extremely friable and very
difficult to prepare for examination under the microscope. The
bones were, of course, recognizable, but they were broken in a
number of places. It is probable that some of the damage to the

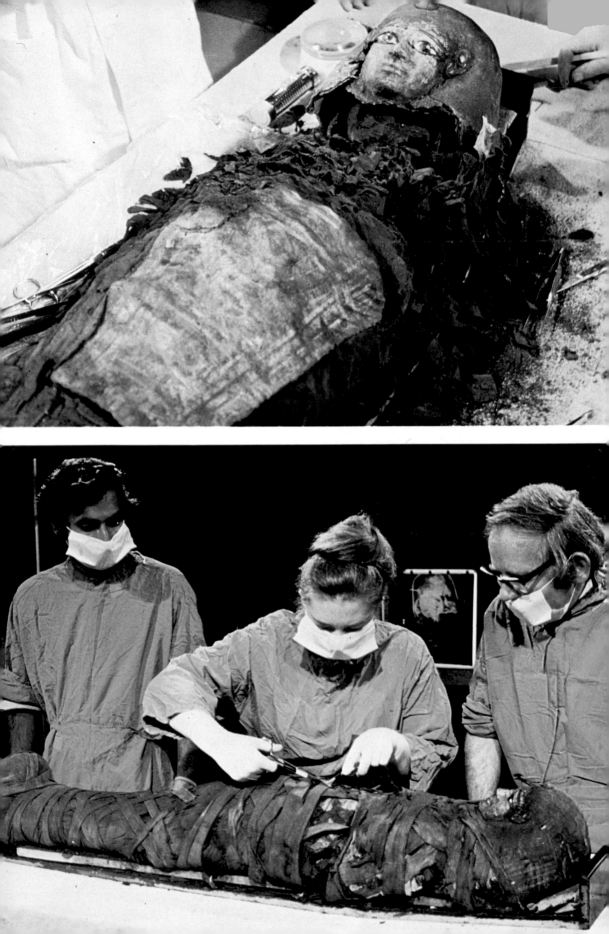

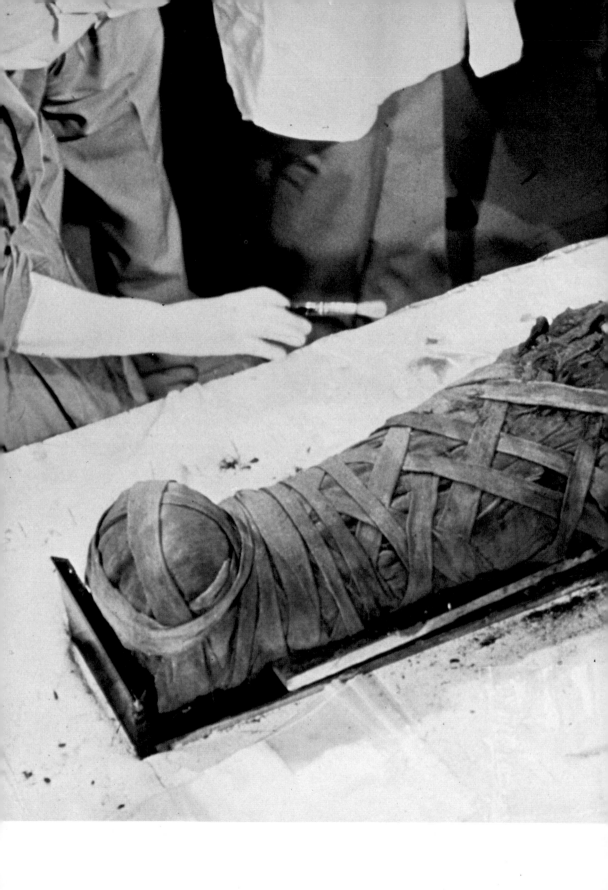

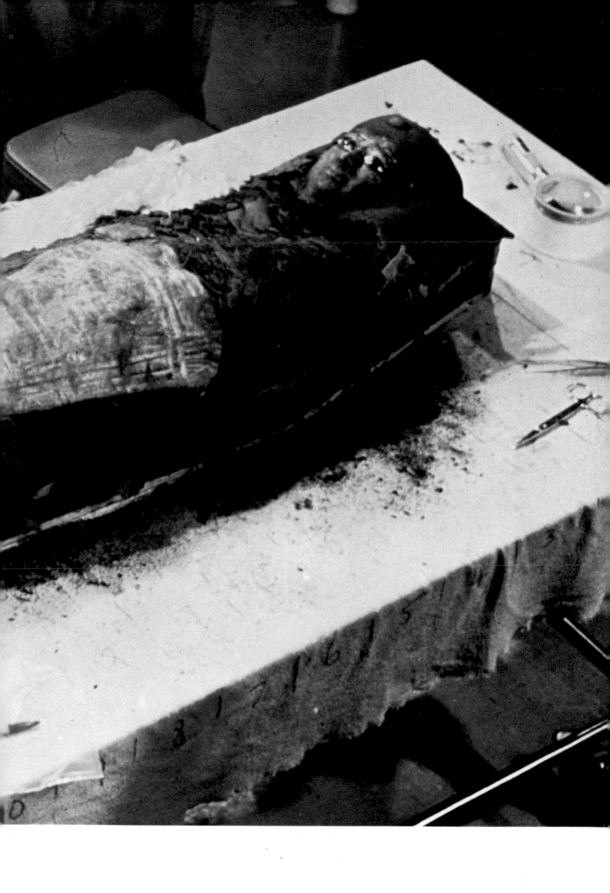

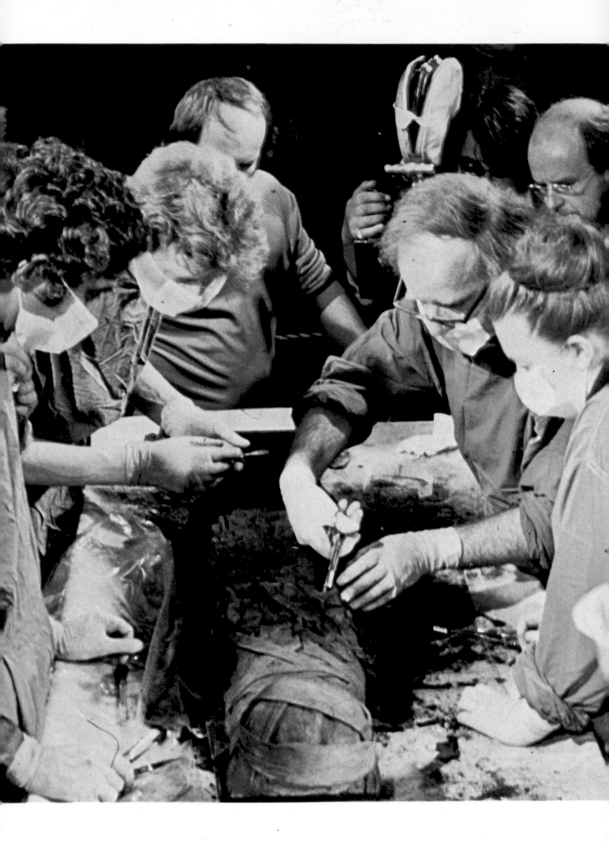

head and to the pelvis was due to earlier lack of care in handling the mummy. There is no positive evidence from the autopsy that the bones were broken during the life of the girl. When bone is broken during life, tissue known as callus forms at the site of the fracture, producing a mass around it and holding the bones together until healing has occurred. A callus is easily recognizable in fresh autopsies and indicates that the fracture occurred during life. Unfortunately, callus sufficiently dense to have remained through the ages at the fracture site would take a few weeks to develop. Consequently, in this case one cannot exclude the possibility that the fracture had occurred round about the time of death, or even a week or two before. Some damage to the head and neck was almost certainly caused at the time that the cartonnage mask was broken, probably by the action of tomb robbers in antiquity. Further evidence for this is seen in the absence of eye-covers, amulets, or other objects around the neck, although gold finger-stalls were present on the fingers and gold nipple-shields on the chest.

The amputation of the legs presented a more difficult problem and is a matter for speculation. There is no evidence of callus at the ends of the bones which indicated that amputation occurred either a short time before death, at the time of death, or after death. Deliberate mutilation during life, the hypothesis put forward before the unwrapping, could not be ruled out. But, of course, one possible reason for mutilation could be discounted as a result of the unwrapping, for the 'foetal head' was found to consist of the artificial feet and slippers. The possibility that the legs had been cut off accidentally during life had also to be considered. Falling masonry, for example, has been reported to have caused injury in ancient Egypt and it was wondered if this child might have had her legs amputated in this kind of accident.

The likelihood that amputation of the legs occurred after death also had to be considered. It is known that there was a certain amount of carelessness in the embalmers' workshops where mummification took place, and it is believed that occasionally limbs were accidentally lost from the bodies during mummification. This was an unlikely explanation, however, for it would have required considerable force, and a deliberate intention, to amputate the limbs through the bones.

There is evidence, as we shall see later, of marked decomposition of the tissues at the time of mummification, and one explanation of this could have been that the body had been in water for some time after death. A body decomposing in a river such as the Nile would be liable to attack. A hippopotamus might well decide to take a bite from such a floating object and certainly crocodiles would do so. It was suggested that the marks

Members of the team and BBC camera crew around the mummy towards the end of the operation

on the end of the bones were the teeth-marks of crocodiles, but it was also pointed out that crocodiles, rather than biting through a bone, often hold on to a limb and shake it until it is disarticulated at a joint. The true cause of the amputation of this poor child's legs had to remain a mystery.

There were a number of features which suggested that the poor state of preservation might have been due to the body being in a fairly advanced state of decomposition when mummification took place. Comments have been made on the almost complete absence of soft tissues. A good deal may have been consumed by insects feeding on the body after death, but this was felt unlikely to be the full explanation. It was interesting to note that the bandages on the legs near the amputation were apparently applied directly to the bone, indicating that there was no soft tissues on the limb at this time.

The absence of the internal organs of the body was also interesting. It was customary for the embalmers to remove some of these, usually the liver, left lung, stomach, and intestines, to be preserved separately, either in canopic jars or placed back in the abdomen as separate packages. None of the organs could be found and while the thoracic cavity was completely empty, the abdomen and pelvis were packed with mud and bandages. So complete a removal of the organs by the embalmers would be extremely rare and their absence again suggested decomposition of the body at the time of wrapping. Moreover, some of the bones of the left leg above the level of amputation were missing. These included the knee-cap and the fibula, a bone which normally lies adjacent to the tibia in the lower part of the leg. These bones are normally attached firmly to the ligaments around the knee and would only become separated if these ligaments had been softened by decomposition.

A further point of interest which indicated decomposition of soft tissues on the head at the time of embalming was the presence of blue and red paint on the skull bones. Clearly, for the skull bones to be painted in this way, very little of the normal soft tissues of the scalp must have been present.

A most intriguing mystery also surrounded the presence of the gold nipple-shields – indicating that the embalmers considered they were dealing with a girl – together with the finding of an artificial phallus, something that they would normally supply for a male mummy. There did not appear to be any simple answer to this, unless the embalmers did not know the sex of the body and were playing safe by providing both male and female attributes for the after-life. If this were true, it was certainly in keeping with the hypothesis that the body was in an advanced state of decomposition at the time of mummification.

 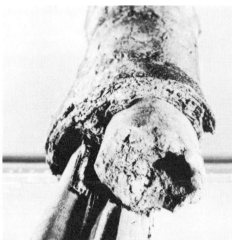

Above: A detail
showing the end of
one of the legs with
the pieces of wood
which splinted it to
the artificial limb.
Above right: The end
of the bone of the
amputated leg.
It was the absence
of callus here which
suggested that the
fracture had occurred
round the time of or
shortly before death

Although insufficient evidence exists to confirm without doubt
the sex of this adolescent, certain features favour its identification as a female and it is subsequently referred to as such.

There were two ways in which the body might have reached
this stage of decomposition. The first concerned the practice
common at this period in ancient Egypt, of allowing girls and
young women to putrefy for a few days before allowing the
embalmers to take away the body. This was done, as might be
anticipated, because there were unfortunately necrophiliacs
among the embalming fraternity. However, it is difficult to see
how so short a period of putrefaction would result in such
marked decomposition. The second and more likely suggestion
was that the child died, and the body was either hidden or lay
undiscovered for some time after death. While this could have
occurred, say, if she had been buried under masonry in an
accident, or if she had been murdered and then hidden, it was
also possible that the body lay in water after death. Water is
essential for putrefaction, and in the dry Egyptian climate the
process of decay takes much longer in a dry body than in one left
in water. Finally, if the body of an unknown young person were
found under some rubble, or pulled out of the Nile in an
advanced state of decomposition, one might ask why the
Egyptians should take such great care in reconstituting the
limbs and feet, and in fitting the body with gold finger-stalls and
nipple-shields. One theory was that she had been in water and
had been partly eaten by crocodiles. The Egyptians believed that
the crocodiles were gods and that anyone who had been food for
them was sacred.

The mystery of these various inconsistencies, and speculation
about their causes went on for some time after the unwrapping

of 1770. It was about a year later, however, when the results of the Carbon-14 dating of the bones and bandages became available, that some of the peculiar findings in 1770 could be understood more readily.

These results provided one of the most surprising and exciting discoveries of the investigation, for they showed that the bones date from over a thousand years before the bandages. By this process the bandages could be dated to the later period of Roman occupation of Egypt, and it would therefore appear that the body dates from a period between the 2nd Intermediate Period and Dynasty XIX. The bandages and associated decorations, including the sandals and nipple-covers, are from this later period; there is no apparent evidence of the original and much earlier wrapping which would have been placed around the mummy when it was treated immediately after death.

The Carbon-14 dating results having shown that a rewrapping took place at a much later date, this provided possible solutions to several of the puzzling questions which had arisen from the unwrapping. It is probable that much of the original tissue and wrappings of the body were lost when the wrappings were removed, which explains our difficulty in finding any tissue. The rewrapping would also explain the presence of resin in some of the joints and between the bones of the spine, even though there is very little in the rest of the wrappings. It would appear that a type of resin producing the discolouration of the cartilage in the bones and spine was used in the initial wrapping, while a different type was employed when 1770 was rewrapped some thousand years later. The poor state of preservation and the lack of tissue is certainly in keeping with the body having been damaged by water, and we shall see later that the presence of insects in the wrappings of mummy 1770 is compatible with the body having been rehydrated shortly before rewrapping was carried out.

However, although possible solutions had been provided to the initial questions, another problem now arose. The careful reconstruction and rewrapping of 1770 in the late Roman period, which provided the deceased with gilded nipple-shields, finger-stalls, decorated sandals, and artificial legs and a foot, suggested that the Egyptians knew that this was someone of considerable importance. However, the provision of both male and female attributes indicates that the embalmers at this second wrapping of 1770 did not know if they were dealing with the body of a man or of a woman. There is evidence that royal mummies were sometimes moved to new tombs, and if damaged, they were attended to by the priests of later generations. We can only suppose that the circumstances of

location in which 1770 was found led the embalmers of the later
period to assume that this was a person of considerable
importance, and although the sex and identity could not be
determined, the body was nevertheless rewrapped in an
elaborate manner, with the inclusion of funerary objects and
artificial limbs to ensure the use of all faculties in the next
world. Unfortunately, the question 'Who was 1770?' cannot be
answered.

The wrappings of mummy 1770

The unwrapping of an Egyptian mummy is an infrequent event
and on such occasions human curiosity ensures that the contents
of the mummy are likely to be of greater interest than the
external wrappings. A considerable amount has already been
written about the bandaging material used by the ancient
Egyptians to wrap the mummified bodies of their dead, and
about the materials which were used to impregnate the bandage
in an attempt to preserve the body. However, the rarity of an
unwrapping does demand that full advantage is taken of the
opportunity to examine and describe as many details of the
mummy as possible, and for this reason an investigation of the
bandages of mummy 1770 was undertaken. One of the aims of
the whole project was to examine the possible role of modern
scientific techniques in the study of Egyptology. In this context
it was hoped that the use of modern techniques might confirm or
refute earlier findings, or even indicate the use of substances not
previously described, possibly because of their presence in
previously undetectable amounts.

The ancient Egyptians depended upon plants, animals, and
minerals to supply everyday needs. Useful substances like glue,
preservatives, perfumes, and medicines all originated from these
sources. However, natural products are complex, and their
identification demands comparatively sophisticated methods of
analysis. Methods currently available to the investigator include
chromatography in its various forms (paper, thin-layer, gas-
liquid), iron-exchange techniques and spectroscopy, all of which
were used in this study. No attempt will be made here to burden
the reader with details of these techniques, but the results of the
research and the various substances found can be seen in the
illustrations on pages 104 and 105.

The bandages of 1770 were, for the most part, in a poor state of
preservation, and this presented an obstacle to any systematic
unwrapping of the mummy. It is noteworthy that in contrast to
previously described mummies, no large fragments of dried
plants or plant extracts were found either among the bandages or

THE INVESTIGATION

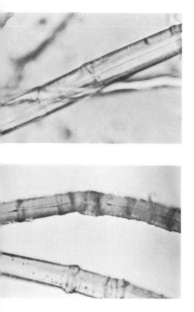

A comparison of fibres taken from the wrappings of 1770 (top) with modern linen (flax) fibre. Interesting details of the former include thickened fibre walls, narrow central cavity, and 'beat marks'

in the body cavities. Small fragments of plant material, including pieces of grass, leaf, flower, and fruit were indeed found among the wrappings of 1770, but it was generally agreed that these were accidental contaminants rather than deliberate inclusions.

At the outset it was clear that the outer wrappings consisted of strips of material, but when these were removed the inner layers were seen to be in the form of sheets of fabric. At least three textures of cloth had been used to wrap the body. There were both coarsely and finely woven materials, with either single or double threads. Pieces of cloth with stitching and selvedges were also found. The fabric varied in weave-density from coarse (six threads per centimetre), to fine (thirty threads per centimetre). Fragments from various parts of the bandage were examined microscopically and this disclosed the presence of fibres with the appearance and dimensions of flax (linen, *Linum usitatissium* L).

Measurements were made of the diameter of the fibres, which were 12-30 microns (1 micron = 1/1000 millimetre). Other diagnostic features included the narrow cavity running the length of the fibre and the presence of so-called 'beat marks' which are produced during the preparation of flax; stems of the flax plant are soaked in water, then beaten to remove the soft parts of the stem, leaving the separated fibres with transverse markings. The dried fibres are spun and woven into a fabric recognized as linen cloth.

The bandages varied in colour from brown to almost black and were considered to be impregnated, possibly with resin or some other perfume or preservative. However, before attempting to extract and identify the materials used to impregnate the bandages, attention was paid to a feature which had been apparent on a cursory examination: this was the presence of a gum-like substance which was clear and brittle and had obviously been used as an adhesive for the outermost strips of bandage. According to Herodotus, plant gum rather than animal glue was employed to fasten together the bandages of mummies. A probable source of this gum was the acacia plant (*Acacia senegal* Willdenow), which grows in Egypt, and previous investigations have disclosed the use of this gum as an adhesive as early as Dynasty IV. In the event, the gum fragments from the bandages proved to be not of this type. However, it was noted that on boiling with acid an unpleasant odour was produced which suggested the presence of protein. It should be explained that proteins, on heating in acid, break down or 'hydrolyse' to their constituent amino-acids. The amino-acids from the hydrolysed glue were identified by paper chromatography and by ion-exchange analysis and shown to be virtually identical with those produced on hydrolysis of gelatin; indeed, the glue was hardly distinguishable chemically from modern gelatin. Gelatin is prepared by boiling animal skins and bones and evaporating and cooling the result to a hard solid. It was widely used by the ancient Egyptians but its use as an adhesive for mummy wrappings does not appear to have been described previously.

In order to examine the brown substance with which the wrappings were impregnated, samples of the bandages were obtained using a series of different solvents. Pieces of bandage were extracted successively with petroleum-ether, chloroform, methanol, and water; fats or waxes would dissolve in the petroleum-ether, while water-soluble substances such as gums would remain until the final loosening of the bandage with water. Pieces of bandages obtained from several different layers around the body were lifted off in this way and the yields of various solvents compared. Up to 40 per cent by weight was lost from some of the bandage samples because of extraction with the solvents, indicating a high degree of impregnation of the fabric.

Extraction of the samples from the outer layers of bandage with petroleum-ether yielded a yellow solution which on removal of the solvent left a waxy residue.

By thin-layer chromatography this extract appeared similar to beeswax. This was in fact confirmed by mass spectrometry of the major components. However, gas-liquid chromatography of the hydrocarbon components revealed that there there are differences between the extract of the bandage and beeswax which suggest the presence of additional hydrocarbon wax substances. There are various possible sources of these hydrocarbons. First, there are some waxes of plant origin which have a similar hydrocarbon pattern on gas-liquid chromatography, but these are known to be obtained from South American species, to which the ancient Egyptians would presumably not have had access. Such plant waxes would show differences from beeswax on thin-layer chromatography and mass spectrometry. Another possible source of the hydrocarbons in the bandage is the natural petroleum wax, ozokerite, readily obtained from the shores of the Dead Sea. Both beeswax and ozokerite are mentioned by Lucas as known to the ancient Egyptians. Beeswax has been found on mummified bodies, though not impregnating wrappings, and ozokerite beads were present in some Egyptian graves, although again there is no report of the use of this material in impregnating mummy bandages.

Earlier investigators have identified various plant resins in mummy wrappings and it could be expected that, if present, these would be extracted by chloroform, rather than petroleum-

Two examples of fabric weave from the wrappings of mummy 1770. Top is a coarse double weave showing double threads in both warp and weft. Below is a fine plain weave with coarse threads introduced at regular intervals

GALBANUM.

Modern examples of the natural products found impregnating the wrappings of 1770. (A) 'Bitumen of Judea' from the Dead Sea; (B) yellow beeswax; (C) leaf gelatin; (D) dried tamarind pods; (E) galbanum

ether, methanol, or water. Examination of the chloroform extract done by thin-layer chromatography suggested the presence of the gum-resin, galbanum (obtained from *Ferula galbaniflua*, Boissier and Bukse), but not myrrh, olibanum (frankincense), storax, colophony, chios turpentine, mastiche, sandarac, ladanum, or bdellium, any of which might have been expected on the basis of earlier reports of their use by the ancient Egyptians in mummification or perfumery. Galbanum is strongly fragrant and might thus be expected to be useful when wrapping the dead. According to Lucas, although galbanum was mentioned by both Pliny and Dioscoroides as an ingredient of Egyptian toiletries and ointments, there is no record of its having been found in Egyptian graves. Further evidence for the presence of galbanum was obtained by paper chromatography, which demonstrated the presence of the sugars galactose and arabinose, characteristic of galbanum. Umbelliferone, a constituent of galbanum, was also detected in bandage extracts by thin-layer chromatography.

The word 'mummy' is derived from the Arabic word for bitumen and has been used to describe the embalmed, wrapped

bodies of ancient Egyptians, presumably because of the black, pitch-like appearance of such bodies. However, there is scant evidence for the presence of bitumen in mummies, and it has been suggested that the blackened appearance is due to the presence of oxidized resin. Lucas suggests that on the basis of available evidence, bitumen was not used during the mummification process until a very late period in Egyptian history, and goes on to postulate that if a greater number of mummies of a late date were examined, the presence of bitumen might be demonstrated. The findings in this study tend to confirm the observations of Lucas in this respect. A probable source of bitumen for the ancient Egyptians was the Dead Sea where 'bitumen of Judea' can be found floating on the water and is easily collected. Bitumen is associated with oil-bearing strata in the earth's crust and consists largely of hydro-carbons, but there are traces of sulphur and also certain heavy metals. The trace metals in 'bitumen of Judea' are nickel, vanadium, and molybdenum.

The early evidence that bitumen might be present in the wrappings of 1770 was obtained by heating to red heat fragments

Examples of the extracts removed from the bandages by various solvents. (A) Chloroform extract; (B) Methanol extract; (C) Petroleum ether extract from the outer layers which analysis showed to be beeswax; (D) Petroleum ether extract from the inner layers, which was shown to be beeswax mixed with galbanum which gave it an orange colour

of bandage with sodium carbonate. A 'metallic mirror' was formed on the inside of the crucible, a possible indication of the presence of metals, and the addition of acid to the residue liberated hydrogen sulphide gas, demonstrating the presence of sulphur. Following this initial observation, samples of bandage were examined for the presence of trace metals by atomic-absorption spectroscopy and neutron-activation analysis. The results of this examination, compared with those obtained on examination of an authentic sample of Dead Sea bitumen, led to the conclusion that bitumen was present in the inner layers of the wrappings.

Significant weights of methanol-soluble and water-soluble extracts were obtained from the bandages. These extracts would not have been found had only bitumen, galbanum, and beeswax been present, since these would have been mostly removed by petroleum-ether and chloroform. As no protein could be detected, dissolved gelatin was also absent. Solutions of the methanol and water extractives in water were acidic, suggesting the possible presence of acidic plant extracts. Lucas refers to the use in perfumery of bitumen mixed with tamarind, a fruit pulp containing considerable amounts of tartaric acid. This pulp, which is found in the pods of the tamarind tree, has a pleasant, fruity odour and thus might have been used to perfume the wrappings of the dead. Unfortunately, thin-layer chromatographic comparison of extracts of tamarind and bandage samples, while indicating some general similarity, did not conclusively demonstrate the presence of tartaric acid in the bandage extracts. Thus the use of tamarind in the impregnation of the bandages remains only a possibility.

The study of the wrappings of 1770 was beset with several problems. First, the material extracted and analysed was probably a complex mixture of natural substances, themselves mixtures, not all of which have been identified in the present study. Secondly, it is possible that chemical changes due to the effects of air, warmth, or moisture, have occurred over hundreds of years, rendering some substances unrecognizable, despite the use of modern techniques. Despite these hazards, one might have expected to find some evidence for the presence of myrrh, olibanum, gum arabic, spices, or other substances, as reported by previous investigators, but no indication of these materials was forthcoming.

The final conclusion of this part of the investigation was that the mummy was wrapped in linen cloth which had been dipped into either a molten mixture of bitumen and galbanum or some solution containing these. There was evidence to suggest that other substances were present in the mixture, but these could not be identified. The outer layers of bandage were, in addition, impregnated with beeswax (possibly with the addition of some mineral wax) and glued in place with gelatin. These findings were somewhat unexpected in that they differ from previous reports, but all the materials found were well known to the ancient Egyptians.

In general terms, the unwrapping of this mummy had provided information about the body which would otherwise have been unobtainable. This included the discovery of the artificial feet and the sandals, the gilded nipple-covers, and finger- and toe-stalls. It provided an opportunity to investigate in detail the amputated ends of the legs and the calcified Guinea worm. In addition, in the process of unwrapping 1770 the evidence of the uncertain identity and sex of the person became apparent, and finally, the exciting discovery that the body had been rewrapped in antiquity.

By investigating one mummy from the collection in this way, it was possible to apply a whole range of techniques to the examination of the body. Also, certain facts were discovered which could not have been brought to light by any less destructive methods of examination.

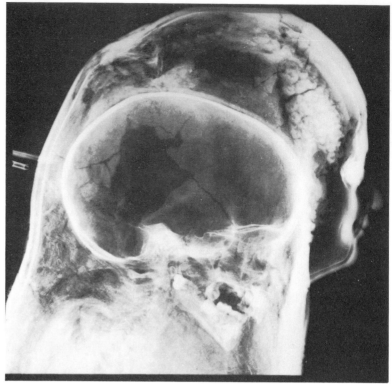

Two x-ray views of the head of a mummy showing that the decorative face on the cartonnage mask is not related in position to the skull inside

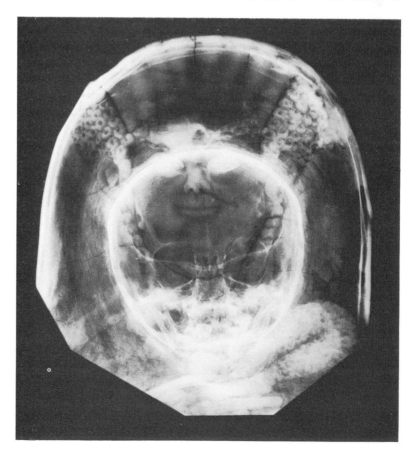

5 The Radiological Examination

THE X-RAY EXAMINATION of mummy 1770 necessarily took place before the unwrapping described in the last chapter, but since all the other mummies were examined radiologically as well, it seems more appropriate to consider them all together here.

The collection of ancient Egyptian mummified remains in Manchester Museum consists of seventeen complete human mummies, a number of loose human appendages, including five heads, and a considerable number of mummified animals and birds. The possibility of investigating radiologically, under near-ideal conditions, the entire collection, and particularly of examining one human mummy (1770), before and after unwrapping, presented a rare scientific opportunity and a unique challenge. All specimens were dealt with in the Department of Neuro-radiology, Manchester Royal Infirmary, where appropriate specialized radiological equipment is available. The investigations were conducted at weekends or at nights, to avoid interfering with patient investigations and possibly alarming the unsuspecting.

The application of modern radiological methods and techniques has allowed the production of radiographs comparable in positioning and in quality with those normally obtained in hospital practice. The objectives of the investigation were to establish standard techniques for other workers to follow, and to record and analyse the radiological data. In the particular case of 1770, it was possible to validate both method and observations by comparing the radiological studies obtained before and after unwrapping.

From the early days of x-rays there was interest in the value of this new 'non-invasive' technique in the investigation of mummified remains. Sir Flinders Petrie probably obtained the first x-ray of a human mummy in 1897, whilst Mr (later Sir) Elliot Smith and Mr Howard Carter tell of their experience in transferring the rigid Pharaoh Tuthmosis VI by taxicab to a private x-ray unit in Cairo in 1904. Among 261 various x-rays obtained in Liverpool in 1896 Thurston Holland illustrates what must be the earliest radiological investigation of mummified remains, a bird (page 111). He observed with some justification that the 'advantage of this class of subject is that there is no movement'. Although mummies have been extensively studied over the years, the scientific value of x-ray investigations in archaeology and Egyptology has only been appreciated in recent years and has been pioneered in particular by the radiologist, Dr P. K. Gray.

Significant advances in x-ray apparatus, methods of image display, and, of course, in medical radio-diagnosis itself have been made during the last eighty years, and it is now inconceivable to think of a hospital without a department of diagnostic radiology. Basic principles of x-ray production and transmission have not changed, but considerable sophistication has been added to the manner in which areas of interest may be explored and the image viewed. The modern x-ray techniques include fluoroscopy, orbiting manoeuvres, and tomography as routine. Fluoroscopy (the transmission of x-rays on to a fluorescent screen) provides an immediate and dynamic view of events to the observer. It is relatively easy to view moving parts or to obtain a three-dimensional image of an object by moving it in the x-ray beam. Ciné or video recordings of the television image are standard practice in modern hospital departments. Detailed investigation of brain disorders in the living has led to the development of specialized radiological equipment capable of orbiting round the subject. Complex engineering has enabled the observer to view the x-ray image, by television link, from an infinite number of angles without moving the subject at all. The nature of the human body is such that features of interest may be partially or even completely obscured by underlying or overlying structures. Tomography is a method of obtaining x-rays of a section or slice of tissue in a plane of interest, rather like taking one card from a pack. This is achieved by blurring out the unwanted shadows above and below the plane of interest, the image of which is then left sharply defined.

When combined with orbiting apparatus and television viewing tomographic facilities offer a versatile and sophisticated method of conducting a radiological examination. Units with this equipment are expensive and are usually located only in highly specialized departments of radiology. Radiological investigation in museums and on archaeological sites is significantly limited by the need for mobile, compact equipment capable of being attached to local electricity supplies. The radiological investigation of mummified remains has been parti-

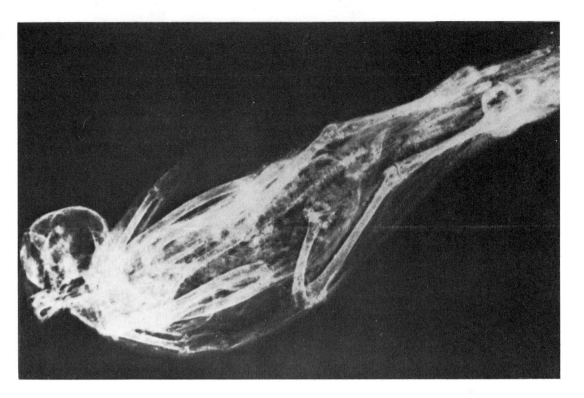

A mummified bird
radiographed by
Dr Thurston Holland
in 1896; this is the
earliest known x-ray of
a mummified object

cularly constrained because of the heavy and dense casing in
which mummy specimens are housed, combined with the problem of artefacts of varying density in the complex wrappings.
There are obvious advantages in being able to conduct the radiological investigation of archeological remains in specialized
radiological departments. Then not only is it possible to 'look
inside' the object by television fluoroscopy, to select the best
radiographic projections, and to obtain the optimum tomographic sections, but it is also possible to take advantage of the
controlled and rapid (e.g., ninety seconds) film processing
facilities immediately available. This, in effect, means taking a
mummy to hospital!

Fluoroscopy (examination by x-rays transmitted on to a
fluorescent screen), was carried out on each subject as a first step
to evaluating the nature of the contents and their disposition.
External modelling and decoration, no matter how elaborate,
has no positional relationship to the anatomical remains within.
Markers were therefore placed on the outer casing of the human
remains to identify the position of certain anatomical features.
As a routine procedure a radiographic survey was then obtained
in two planes, using overlapping films to include the entire
subject; in other words, a basic plan and elevation. These radiographs, together with the fluoroscopic observations, were then
studied to devise a logical and more detailed investigation.
There are two main areas of interest in the x-ray investigation of

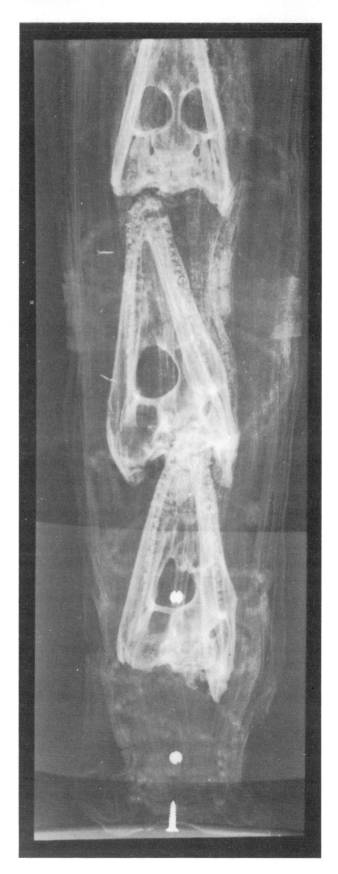

A crocodile-shaped
wrapping was shown to
contain four skulls,
three of which appear
here, rather than
the body of
one of Egypt's
sacred animals

This unpromising object (above left) turned out to be a mummified gerbil with its own haversack of food (left)

human remains, one concerned with the archaeology of the specimen and its relationship to the time-scale of cultural development, and the other with the scientific study of disease and trauma in ancient civilizations. The term palaeopathology has been used for the latter group.

ARCHAEOLOGY The presence or absence of human or animal tissue can usually be determined during a preliminary fluoroscopic examination, although more detailed studies may be necessary to exclude such tissue with certainty. A number of forgeries filled with rubbish have in the past been sold to gullible travellers as genuine ancient Egyptian relics! No such forgeries have been found among the Manchester collection, but elaborate wrappings of authentic origin reputedly containing animal relics have been found quite empty. One relic, ostensibly enclosing a single crocodile, contained instead the heads of four, in tandem (see opposite). These are puzzling artefacts and may, one supposes, in the context of mummified 'pets', be attempts at substitution. A wide variety of such mummified 'pets' has been examined, including birds (usually hawks), crocodiles, cats, and one small rodent, probably a gerbil, equipped with its haversack of food for the life to come. The general state of the

contents, prior to more detailed examination, may suggest interference, damage, or even rewrapping after the original mummification.

X-ray examination presents a unique opportunity in everyday
clinical practice to evaluate skeletal maturity and development.
The formation of bone begins at certain main centres about the
eigth week of pregnancy and progresses at some sites into adult
life. After birth, bony epiphyses, or centres of bone development
begin at one or both of the ends of the long bones. When the
particular bone has reached its adult length these epiphyses fuse
with the remainder of the bone. The time-scale for this bony
development varies in different parts of the body. Fusion of the
various skull bones may not take place until adult life. The skull
of a child may, therefore, readily collapse after death.

Nearly 100 ossification centres (sites of bone development) can
be considered in the skeletal assessment of age in human
beings, but as a basis six body sites are important, the hands,
feet, elbows, knees, shoulders, and hips. Due to overlying structures and varying postures in mummies much detailed tomographic study may be necessary to evaluate the state of bony
development at some of these sites.

Modern well-documented European and North American
radiological standards exist to define bone age with accuracy. It
must be recognized however, when considering the bone age of
an ancient Egyptian mummy, that there may be significant racial
differences as a result of genetic and nutritional factors; there is
a general tendency towards earlier skeletal maturity. To be truly
accurate, radiological standards should not only be of the same
ethnic group, but also of a contemporary population.

Tooth calcification and development, although subject to the
same variations and constraints of interpretation, may offer
additional significant information about individual age. Thick-
section tomography in specially contrived planes calculated from
the initial skull radiographs has been necessary to render this
data accessible.

In a number of mummies the appearance of the genitalia may
enable sex to be determined easily, but where doubt exists it
may be necessary to consider specific skeletal features relating to
size and shape of particular bones, especially the pelvis.
Awareness of the variations and overlaps between the sexes is
important.

Detailed radiological investigation of mummified remains has
enabled considerable information to be gained about the
techniques employed by those responsible for the embalming.
As the processes of mummification developed over the
centuries, from pre-dynastic desiccation in hot sand to the

elaborate stylized ceremonial of the later dynasties, and then final decline after the Roman period, so the radiological observations of today reveal a variety of skeletal and soft-tissue changes. Posture of the subject and particularly the position of the arms and hands may be significant, together with the general disposition and organization of the remains. The arms may be extended and the hands at the sides, resting on the thighs or over the pubic region. When the arms are crossed over the chest the left hand may be clenched, suggesting the Osiris position.

Radiological investigations have been directed towards specific features which might indicate particular embalming techniques. Extensive tomography of the chest and abdominal regions has enabled the presence or absence of intact body organs to be revealed. Removal of body organs, with the exception of the heart and kidneys, was practised as early as Dynasty IV (2613-2494 BC), using an incision in the left flank. The viscera so removed were initially placed in canopic jars, but at a later period were replaced in packages in the body cavity or

Radiology has proved useful in identifying the sex of mummies – or exposing a fraud. Here a false phallus – similar to that associated with 1770 – shows clearly on the x-ray

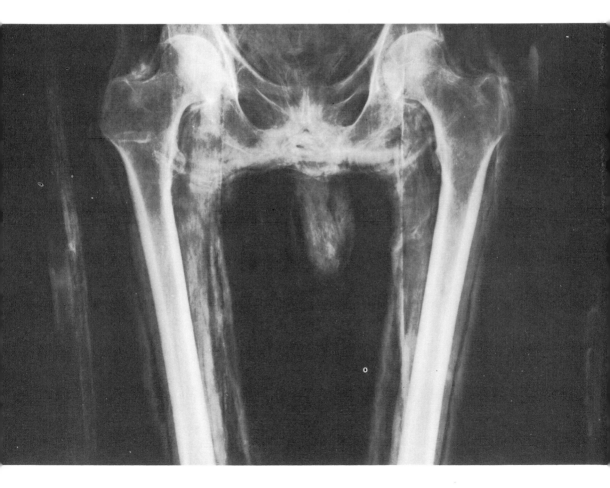

A preliminary
radiographic survey of
this reed coffin (top)
showed the skeleton of
the baby (above)

between the legs. The heart has been readily identifiable by tomography but, unexpectedly in two subjects, collapsed lungs have also been revealed in the chest cavity. Tomography has also made it possible to distinguish between packages of organs and overlying artefacts.

Particular attention has been directed towards the head in order to define the site of removal of the brain. At the peak of the art of mummification in Dynasty XXI (1069-945 BC) the brain was removed via the nose, as described by Herodotus. The insertion of a metal instrument into the cranial cavity through the nostril inevitably resulted in a fracture of the thin aerated bone separating the nasal cavity from the brain. This technique, which incidentally is very similar to one used at the present time as a surgical procedure to remove some tumours of the pituitary gland, must have been carried out with particular skill. The bony defect is often impossible to detect without the use of very thin section tomography or stereoscopy.

During the dynastic periods the body was treated with natron, a mixture of salts including sodium carbonate and sodium bicarbonate, as a preservative. Natron was replaced in the Ptolemaic period (332-30 BC) largely by molten resin which was poured into the various body or cranial cavities. At the same time considerably less care was taken of the body and more attention

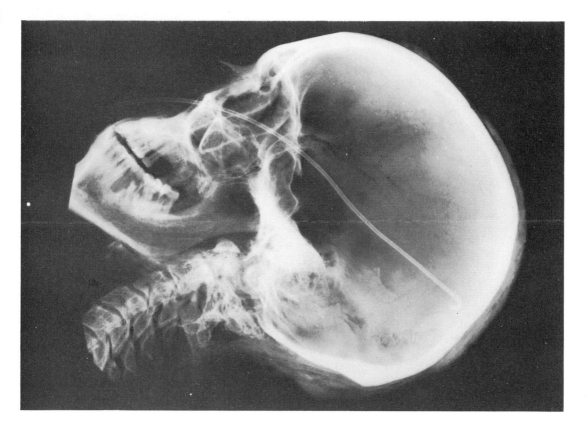

given to the elaborate wrappings. Resin within the skull is detectable as a mass of increased density which may exhibit limiting features suggesting that membranes normally supporting the brain are still present.

A mummified skull with a modern, radio-opaque catheter inserted through the nose to show how the brain was removed

Amulets of religious significance were often placed in the wrappings and being made of ceramic or metal, sometimes gold, are easily detected radiologically. A rectangular plate has also on occasions been demonstrated overlying the left flank incision on the body.

PALAEOPATHOLOGY   This section of the study was directed towards detecting evidence of disease in both the bony skeleton and the remaining soft tissue and, where possible, the character of the disease. In addition, evidence of trauma has been sought, and possible causes of death.

Growing bone is extremely sensitive to temporary illnesses and to periods in bed. The growing end of the bone ceases to grow temporarily but continues to lay down calcium. When the patient recovers, and the normal pattern of bone development resumes, the line of 'arrested growth' may remain as a clear, dense, transverse line and show on a radiograph. The distance of the line from the end of the bone can then be used to give an estimate of the person's age at the time of illness. It may be

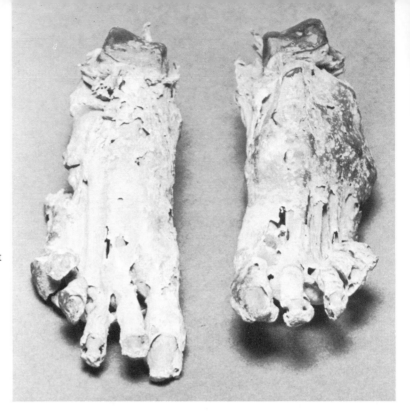

When the mummified feet of Khnum Nakht (right) were re-examined radiologically (below) it was discovered that he had not suffered from a club foot as had been suspected in 1906. The appearance of the left foot was due to tight bandaging

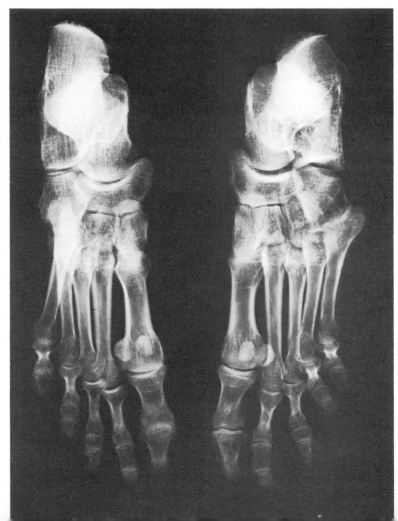

possible to make observations about the general state of health of the individual during this period of bone growth.

Adult bones and joints subject to the normal wear and tear of everyday living, accentuated by osteo-arthritis, frequently exhibit evidence of degeneration. Such change is shown by the development of bony spurs and thickenings near to joints under stress. The joints themselves may become narrowed. These findings are most frequently observed in the spine, the hips, and the hands, and do not appear to differ in distribution or frequency from ancient Egypt to the present day. The only bone tumour to be demonstrated in this collection of mummies was a small bone cyst associated with the right humerus in one case. Such a cyst may have given rise to intermittent pain in the arm but would not have contributed to the cause of death. Fractures and dislocations have been discovered in many mummies but most were not in places normally prone to injury and were probably due to damage after death. One mummy did, however, have a pelvic fracture, which had all the manifestations of an injury sustained during life, and could well have been a contributory factor to the individual's death.

Two of the Manchester mummies, known as the Two Brothers, were unwrapped and subjected to close scrutiny in 1906, by Dr Murray, although neither has undergone extensive radiological investigation until the present day. Only the bony skeletons now remain. One brother, Nekht Ankh, was considered by the original investigators to have eunuch-like features and the present radiological survey only serves to confirm these suspicions. Female characteristics are present in the skull, which is smaller and has less well-developed sinuses and superciliary ridges than normal in the male, and they can also be seen in the long bones, which are again smaller, with less well developed ridges of muscle attachment. The second brother, Khnum Nakht, was alleged at the original investigation to have a deformity of the left foot, with skin and tissue thickening indicating a club foot (*talipes varus*). The present radiological studies did not reveal any evidence of arthritis or secondary bone change in the foot which might have been anticipated in a long-standing congenital deformity. This has been debated by several authorities in the past and the present study supports the theory that the findings are due to the excessively tight wrapping after death rather than to a club foot.

A number of disease processes have been discovered in Egyptian mummies by previous research workers, but there has been a notable absence of certain 'modern' diseases such as cancer, syphilis, tuberculosis, and rickets. Stones in the gall bladder and kidney have been reported in Egyptian mummies,

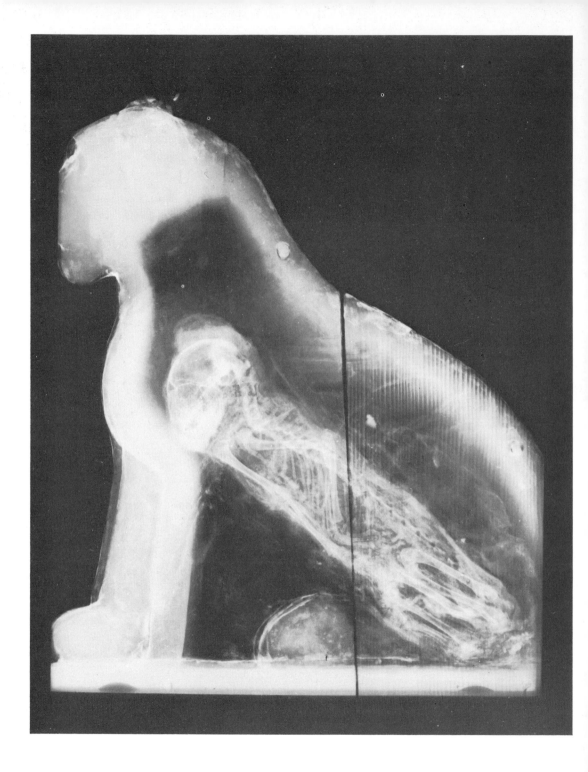

The radiograph (above) of this painted
wooden coffin of a mummified cat (right)
shows the precise position of the corpse

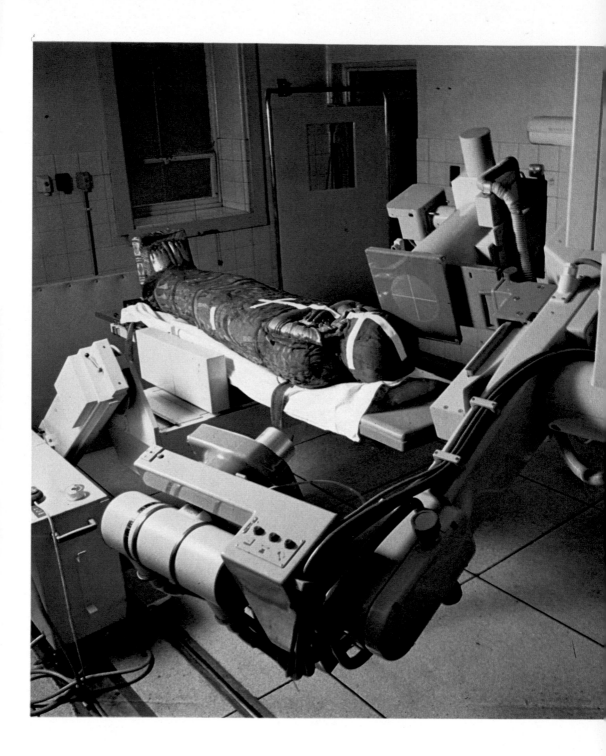

together with calcification in major blood vessels, indicating arterio-sclerosis, but no evidence of these conditions has been found in the present study. Calcification in the abdominal wall of 1770 was observed, and later demonstrated radiologically, to be due to a calcified Guinea worm (p. 124).

MUMMY 1770 Before the unwrapping, a detailed radiological survey was carried out on this mummy. The most striking features were the amputation of the right leg at the mid-shaft of the femur and of the left leg below the knee. The left fibula and patella were absent and there was evidence of erosion of the upper tibia. The missing limbs had been replaced by short artificial limbs each made of amorphous material and fitted with artificial feet. The amputated ends of the bone were of high density but even examination by tomography failed to identify any bone regeneration with certainty. A detached tooth was present in the wrappings of the right leg, suggesting that there had been some disturbance of the remains after embalming. This suspicion was supported by the evident disarray of the ribs and thoracic cage, and also of the disarticulated, collapsed skull. The arms were crossed in front of the chest.

Investigation undertaken by tomography of the key points of the growing skeleton indicated, at least by modern western standards, a person of approximately thirteen to fourteen years old. The growing surfaces of the vertebrae were detached but, in addition, an increased density of the intervertebral disc material was present. No internal organs could be identified at all, but an intriguing dense mass was discovered in the soft tissues over the abdomen.

After unwrapping, all the skeletal remains and a number of other relevant parts, were reinvestigated radiologically, not only to confirm the previous findings but hopefully to enable additional information to be derived. The facial block, for example, although identified before unwrapping, revealed on tomographic examination later an asymmetry of the normal air-containing cavities. No evidence of bone erosion could be detected and the appearances indicate under-development of the left-sided air sinus. Further tomography of the amputated ends of the lower limbs did not reveal any evidence of bone regeneration, nor was there any suggestion of other bone deformity. The amputations might, therefore, have occurred just before or at the time of death rather than as a result of damage after death. The dense mass observed in the abdominal wall was subjected to especial radiological scrutiny and found to contain unequivocal evidence of a calcified Guinea worm, certainly the oldest on record.

One of the Manchester mummies undergoing investigation on the specialised equipment in the Department of Neuro-radiology at Manchester Royal Infirmary

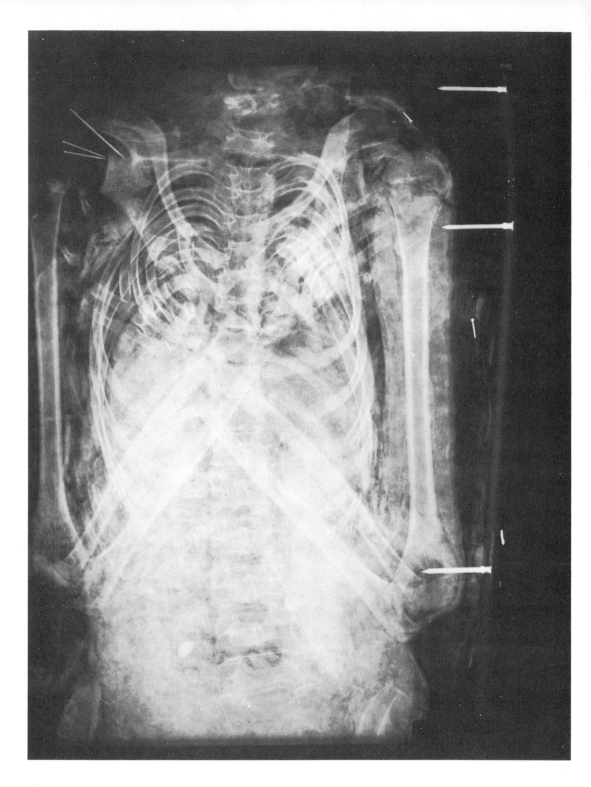

An x-ray of the upper part of mummy 1770 showing the crossed arms
and the small white density over the abdomen which turned out
to be the coiled outline of a calcified guinea-worm

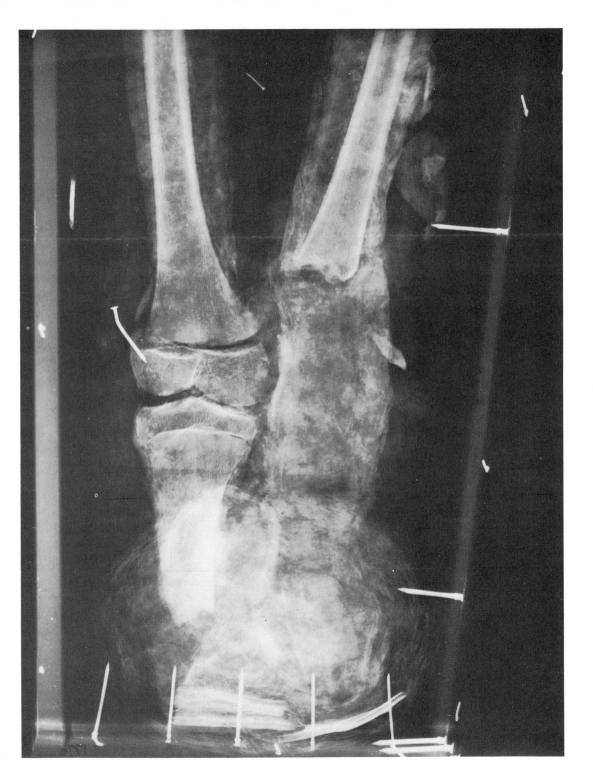

The lower part of mummy 1770 showing the amputated
legs and the indistinct mass which turned out to
be the artificial feet and sandals

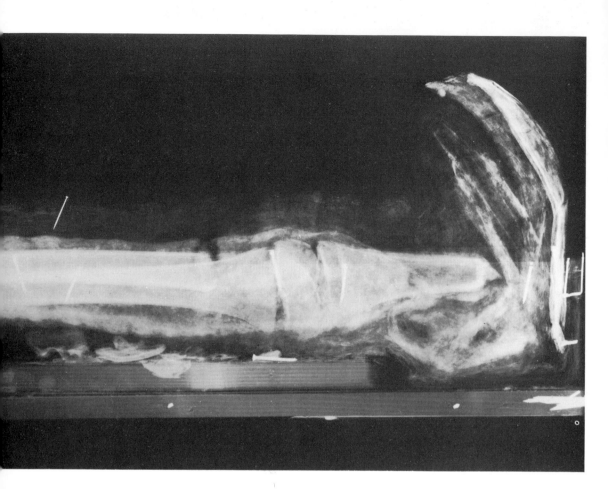

A side view of the artificial legs and feet of 1770

No evidence of mineral colouring could be found on the highly decorative sandals revealed during unwrapping and it must be presumed that they are painted with vegetable pigments. The very thin gold leaf over the finger ends and artificial toes was just demonstrable when examined as specimens radiologically but could not be detected in the wrapped mummy.

The radiological examination of the Manchester mummies was valuable in several ways. It was possible to establish a set of standard techniques under near-ideal conditions at Manchester Royal Infirmary which is close to the Museum. With certain reservations, it made it possible to estimate the age at death of the mummies and to help to establish the sex of each individual. Radiology also added to our knowledge of embalming techniques in ancient Egypt by indicating the position of the arms of the mummies, the presence or absence of the internal body organs, and the way in which the brain had been removed.

126

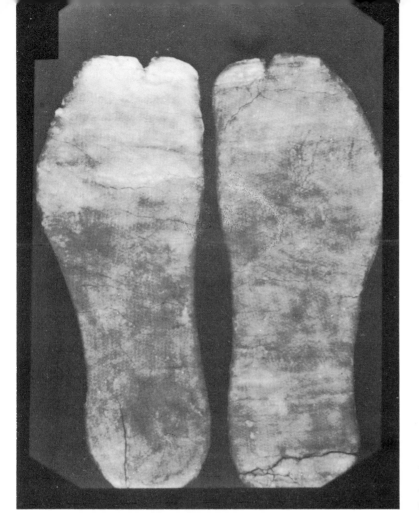

A radiograph of the pair
of decorative sandals,
which did not reveal
any mineral pigment

Again, it showed the presence of amulets placed for magical
protection between the layers of wrapping. In the examination
of any group of mummies, radiological investigation can make a
valuable contribution in establishing evidence of disease both in
the bony skeleton and in the remaining soft tissue. The
character of the disease can sometimes be determined and also
the possible cause of death. This sort of investigation turned out
to be particularly important in the examination of the mummies
of the Two Brothers and of 1770, both before and after
unwrapping.

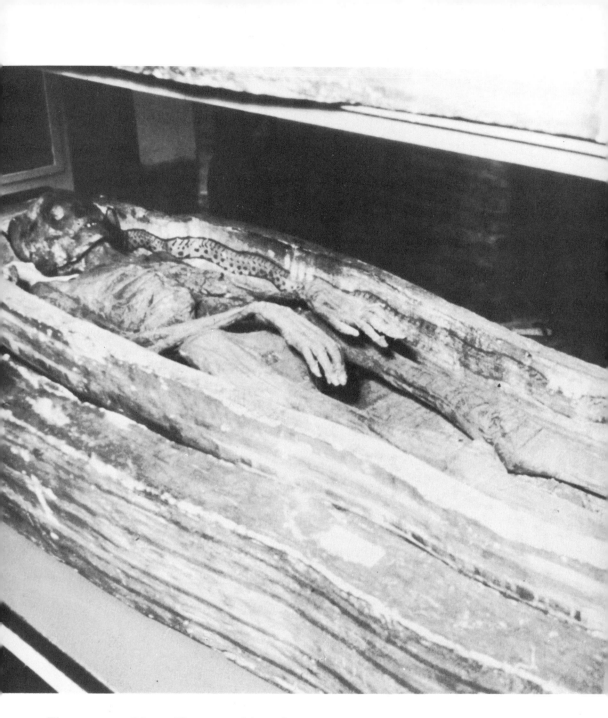

The mummy of Asru, 'Chantress of Amun',
which provided some of the most interesting
material for histological examination

6 The Pathology of the Manchester Mummies

A PERSON WHO STUDIES DISEASE is known as a pathologist. There are obviously many kinds of pathologist, but the person most familiar to the general public is the hospital pathologist, who studies disease and helps in diagnosing diseases which affect human beings. He may be thought of chiefly as the person who does post-mortem examinations but in fact in addition to the dissection of the body after death, there is a wide range of techniques which he may apply in different fields of pathology. It was these techniques that it was hoped to apply in the study of the Manchester mummies and it is, therefore, worthwhile to look briefly at some of them.

The section of pathology dealing with disease produced by organisms invading the living body is known as bacteriology, although in addition to disease caused by bacteria, it encompasses a whole range of organisms varying in size from tape worms measuring many feet in length to the smallest virus, which can be visualized only when magnified many thousand times under the electron microscope. The main objective of the bacteriologist is to identify the offending organism so that the patient may be given the appropriate treatment. To do this he searches under the microscope for the organisms in the tissues, and also attempts to grow (culture) them in special media which encourages their multiplication. It was in connection with the bacteriology of the mummies that face masks were worn by the team during the unwrapping. In the first place, it was hoped to attempt to culture any organisms which might have been lingering beneath the wrappings, for it has been shown that some disease-producing organisms may persist in dry conditions for many years. By using face masks there was less chance of contaminating the tissues by modern bacteria escaping from the mouth or nose of members of the team. In addition, the masks were worn to protect the members of the team from inhalation of harmful organisms which might be lurking in the mummy dust. It is interesting, from this point of view, to remember that the so-called 'curse of the mummies', and in particular the death of a number of Egyptologists shortly after opening tombs, has been blamed recently by one group of research workers on breathing in a pathogenic fungus (one which can cause disease) which has been found in the passage leading to some of the tombs. Attempts to culture organisms from the mummies were unsuccessful but numerous organisms, some of them pathogenic, have been found by direct microscopy of the tissues.

Chemical pathology is the study of changes in the chemical composition of the body tissues. It has made great strides in the past few years, and many techniques are becoming available which could be used in the study of mummified tissue. Few of these techniques have been used so far, although the presence of trace elements (substances found in minute amounts in the body) has been examined using the electron microscope and will be dealt with later. Research workers in America, however, have explored this field further and have carried out interesting work on the composition of the proteins and fats in mummified tissue.

Haematology is the branch of pathology concerned with disease caused by alterations in the number and type of the cells found in the blood. It is probable that the ancient Egyptians were affected by dietary deficiencies which would produce anaemias, and they certainly suffered from schistosomiasis, a disease which results in anaemia due to continuous blood loss from the bladder. Red cells, however, are not easy to find in mummified tissue, and probably some of those which have been described in the past were in fact the spores of fungi and not red cells. Recently, however, research workers in America have shown that by using the electron microscope it is possible to examine the cells of the blood in great detail, and this is one more technique which is now available for the study of disease in mummified tissue. However, the main tool which has been available to pathologists for the greater part of this century is still the one which is the most valuable in the study of disease in the mummies. This is the histological examination of the tissue, which involves the preparation of very thin slices of tissue and their examination under the light microscope. Electron-microscopy of the tissue which is an extension of this technique, using electrons instead of light, will be dealt with at the end of the chapter.

The histo-pathologist, of course, normally deals with fresh tissue taken either at surgical operation or at autopsy. The tissue is usually placed first in a solution of formalin. This process is known as fixation. It inhibits any enzyme activity in the tissue and kills any organism which might be present, and as a result prevents decomposition of the tissue. Now the mummification process that the Egyptians carried out also fixed the tissue, but in this case by dehydrating it to such an extent that the enzymes and bacteria normally responsible for decomposition were prevented from their normal destructive function. Unfortunately, in addition to preserving the disease, dehydration, as one might expect, makes the tissue very hard and brittle. Moreover, the hardness of the tissue is often increased by the presence of resins that the Egyptians sometimes used to aid preservation. It is, therefore, the fragility and hardness of mummified tissue that the pathologist must first overcome before he can prepare histological sections.

Some of the earliest attempts to overcome this problem were carried out by Dr Marc Armand Ruffer, Professor of Pathology at Cairo University, shortly after the First World War. He experimented with a number of rehydrating solutions, but usually used sodium carbonate to soften the tissue before fixing it with formalin. In the present work, after a good deal of trial and error, it was found that combined rehydration and fixation with a 5 per cent formol saline solution was the most satisfactory.

Once rehydration and fixation have been carried out then particular care must still be taken to prevent disintegration of the tissue while it is passed through various alcoholic solutions and finally embedded in paraffin wax. The wax holds the tissue together and enables thin sections to be cut on a machine known as a microtome. The sections are placed on a glass slide, the wax dissolved away and various dyes applied to the sections, which selectively colour (stain) different tissues and cellular components. These dyes have, of course, been developed over the years to stain tissues from surgical operations and autopsies and, as might be expected, they do not always successfully stain tissue which is between 2,000 and 4,000 years old; thus other dyes must often be used.

Coming now to disease revealed by histological study, there were four mummies from which tissues for histological examination were available. The first of these was Nekht Ankh, one of the Two Brothers, who lived during Dynasty XII and was about sixty years of age when he died. Very little tissue remained attached to his bones when the bandages were removed, most of it falling into fairly small fragments. These fragments were gathered together and stored carefully in a glass container, and it was in this state that the author found them some seventy years later. Some of the fragments were recognizable as parts of the ribs. More interesting, however, were the fragments of soft tissue attached to some of these ribs, for these were seen

A piece of mummified lung tissue from Nekht-Ankh, one of the Two Brothers, before (top) and after rehydration with formol saline

under the microscope to be parts of the lung. The lung tissue was not normal but appeared to be damaged by the presence of large scars consisting of fibrous tissue (see page 133). However, the amount of lung in these fragments was small and difficult to interpret.

It was fortunate, therefore, that the canopic jars from the tomb of Nekht Ankh have also been preserved, and when these were investigated histologically it was discovered that one of them contained further lung tissue. This material was extremely hard, quite unlike normal lung tissue, but after rehydration structures could be recognized. Histological sections showed partly collapsed lung in which many of the blood vessels were surrounded by fine black particles. They also showed scarred areas similar to those seen in the fragments attached to the ribs. Moreover, these scarred areas also contained masses of particles identical with those seen round the blood vessels. The use of special stains showed that the scarred areas contained both fibrous and elastic tissue. When the particles were examined in polarized light it became clear that they were crystalline and had properties similar to those of silica particles.

The overall picture was one of damage to the lung due to the presence of harmful particles and very similar to that seen in the lungs of coal-miners and stone-workers. These men get severe damage to the lung due to the inhalation of small particles containing silica, and it is the silica which causes inflammation in the lungs and subsequent scarring. The electron microscope examination of sections from these lungs will be described later, and it will be seen that a further special technique using this instrument indicated that the particles in the lungs of Nekht Ankh were almost certainly sand particles, basically a stone containing a high silica content. Lesions similar to the one in Nekht Ankh's lungs have been described recently in the lungs of desert people living in both the Sahara and the Negev desert, and are believed to be caused by breathing in fine sand particles. This condition has been called sand pneumoconiosis. It is probable that sand particles are not as dangerous as freshly-broken particles of stone, such as the coal-miner encounters, but sand is nevertheless clearly capable of causing considerable damage to the lung.

The method of his embalming and the inscriptions found by Dr Margaret Murray on his tomb furniture indicate that Nekht Ankh was not a stonemason, although this must have been a fairly common occupation in ancient Egypt. There is little doubt, however, that the whole population would have been subjected at intervals to violent sandstorms of the type that desert populations still have to endure, and that the conditions pro-

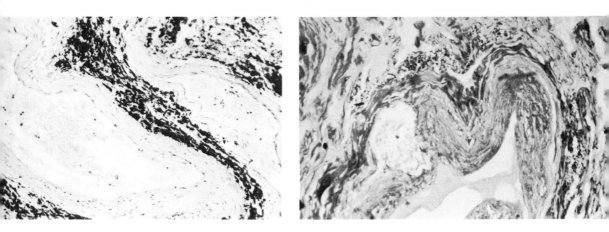

ducing this man's disease are similar to those still endured by people in desert regions to-day.

Sections from some areas of the piece of lung from the canopic jar indicated that Nekht Ankh also had diseases affecting the lungs and heart. These sections show that part of the wall of the heart was removed with the lung and that this was due to the two structures being stuck together. Thus when the embalmer attempted, as was the custom, to remove the lung and leave the heart behind, he found this to be difficult, and he had to take out part of the heart along with the lung. The adhesions between the heart and lung could only be due to pericarditis, a condition where there is inflammation of the surface of the heart. It will be remembered that fragments of the lung were also stuck to the ribs. These adhesions are again a result of inflammation between the chest wall (containing the ribs) and the lung. It would appear, therefore, that in addition to suffering from sand pneumoconiosis Nekht Ankh had, during his life, suffered from inflammation on the surface of his lung (pleurisy) and heart (pericarditis). These two conditions would almost certainly be the result of an attack of pneumonia, but it is difficult to say to what extent he was debilitated by these conditions. It is probable, however, that he suffered from breathlessness, particularly if he exerted himself, and he may well have had a severe cough. Moreover, pain in the chest might well have been a problem, particularly when he took a deep breath or coughed. How he died is largely guesswork, but his lung condition might well have led to his being increasingly a respiratory cripple, and ultimately to his death. Alternatively, the strain on his heart due to the damaged lungs may well have become too severe and he would then have died of heart failure.

Asru, Dynasty XXI-XXV, lies in a glass case on the first floor of the Manchester Museum, and when she was unwrapped some years ago a mass of material was found lying between her legs.

A comparison between lung tissue taken from Nekht Ankh (above left) and a modern coal miner (above) showing a similar condition with fine particles (dark areas) grouped around a blood vessel. Both are magnified 120 times

133

This looked most unpromising, but again a histological examination has proved to be most interesting. The section showed that the mass consisted of stomach and intestines and that the latter were affected by a worm infestation. The worms were in both the mucosa (lining of the intestine) and the muscular wall of the intestine, and appear to have been the cause of significant disease. Here again the electron microscope was a help in identifying the organism as a nematode worm, probably *Strongyloides*, and the details of this work is described on pages 138–43.

Strongyloides is a very interesting parasite found in many tropical and semi-tropical countries, as well as in more northerly latitudes. The life cycle of these worms is extremely complicated but, in general, immature forms of the worm gain access to the body through the skin when this comes into contact with contaminated soil. From the skin the young worms pass along the veins and eventually reach the lungs. There they mature into adult worms which then travel up the airways as far as the pharynx where they are swallowed and hence reach the stomach and intestines. Here the female lays eggs which are passed in the stools; these eggs are eventually hatched out in the soil, where they remain, ready to start the cycle again.

It is clear even from this simplified life cycle that the disease will persist in conditions where hygiene is poor and where the soil is contaminated with faeces. Certainly it would have been prevalent among the lower classes in ancient Egypt. On the other hand, it is believed that Asru was a noblewoman and it would appear, therefore, that the disorder occurred in all levels of society. The infestation would certainly have given Asru stomach-ache and she may well have had diarrhoea, with probably some blood in the stools. In addition, of course, as the worm spends part of its life cycle in the lung, where it causes inflammation, she might well have had a cough with some wheezing, symptoms rather like those found in the asthma sufferers of today. Whether they caused her death is a matter for speculation, but it is known that occasionally the worm produces a particularly severe inflammation in the large bowel and rectum, and from there the worms spread to many other parts of the body and result in death. A complete examination of the whole body might well throw some light on whether this had occurred in Asru's case, but unfortunately this would involve more interference with the body than the members of the team feel is justified at the present time.

Evidence of a different parasitic worm causing disease in ancient Egypt was discovered during the unwrapping of 1770, for a small hard nodule found in the anterior abdominal wall was proved by radiography to be the calcified remains of a Guinea worm (*Dracunculus medinensis*). Infection with this worm is still common in some parts of the Near East, Africa, and India. Like the *Strongyloides* is has a complicated life cycle but is picked up by man as a result of drinking water in which there is a small crustacean containing immature forms of the worm. These are liberated from the crustacean by the gastric juices and the immature worms migrate through the wall of the stomach and mature into adults in the anterior abdominal wall. The male worm is small and dies after fertilizing the female. It is probable that the worm found in 1770 is in fact a male. When a worm dies in the body tissues, calcium salts are deposited in the corpse and it is in fact these salts which have preserved the outline of the worm in 1770 for the past 3,000 years. The female worm is much larger than the male and may reach up to one yard in length. It wanders through the tissues under the skin and tends to come to rest in the legs or feet, where eggs are laid. Here it causes ulceration of the skin and the eggs are released through the ulcer. Once the eggs get into water they are taken up by crustaceans and the cycle is ready to start again.

During her life 1770 may well have complained of feeling hot (there is often a fever) and of severe itching. She probably had a skin rash rather like the present day nettle-rash. All these symptoms are due to the body becoming allergic to the presence of the worms under the skin. Attempts are usually made to remove the worm; one old method consisted of holding one end of the worm as it emerged from the ulcer in the skin, and attaching it to a cleft stick, the thickness of a pencil. The worm was carefully wound on to the stick by turning the latter slowly round and hopefully the whole worm could be extracted in this way. If the large female worm should die before it is removed then a severe inflammation occurs in the legs and abcesses are common. It is interesting to speculate that these were so severe in the case of 1770 that the child's legs had to be amputated surgically. Although this is a possibility, the appearance of the ends of the bone did not support this theory and it was later disproved by the evidence from the radio-carbon dating research.

Finally, to move on to a different kind of disease, a mummified head (mummy No 7740) proved interesting in that a good deal of the brain had been left behind during mummification and it was possible to examine histological sections of this tissue. In one area within the brain the tissue had 'disappeared' leaving a cystic space. The general preservation of the brain was poor and this will be commented on again later, but the appearance of this particular area suggested that the cystic area was not due to autolysis of the tissues after death but was all that remained when that part of the brain had died during life as a result of the blood supply to the area being cut off. The blood supply to any organ is affected when the lumen of the vessel supplying it is narrowed by disease such as artero-sclerosis. This condition is one in which fatty deposits are laid down in the walls of arteries, eventually leading to severe narrowing of the arteries, and obstruction, often associated with clotting of the blood (thrombosis). It has not been possible to examine the blood vessels supplying the brain in the case of 7740, but there is plenty of evidence from other researchers that arterial disease of this type occurred in ancient Egypt. Two interesting examples are worth mentioning: the Pharaoh Merneptah (Dynasty XIX) has been described as having a severely calcified aorta whilst Ramesses II (Dynasty XIX) had a similar condition in his temporal arteries.

The effects produced by the kind of lesion seen in the brain of 7740 depend on the exact part of the brain affected, but in general they come under the general term of a stroke. From their everyday experiences of people who have suffered from strokes, readers will be aware that paralysis of one or more limbs is often present and sometimes the ability to speak is impaired. Whether this man living so many years ago had such a severe effect from his stroke we will never know.

The present studies show that with patience and care, it is quite possible to prepare excellent histological sections with which the normal structures in the tissues of ancient Egyptians may be examined, and from which new evidence can be gained of the diseases from which they suffered.

It has been known for many years that the ancient Egyptians suffered from schistosomiasis, a disease caused by a worm, which starts when the skin is exposed to the mud of the flooded Nile Valley, in which lives a particular type of snail which is the intermediate host and essential for the spread of the disease. The present research indicates that other parasites, such as *Strongyloides*, with rather similar life cycles and also dependent on the contact of the skin with contaminated soil, were also a problem at this time. Moreover, the Guinea-worm infestation from which 1770 suffered is also due to contamination of soil, and hence drinking water, by immature forms of the parasite. It is not surprising that diseases of this type should be prevalent in a country where large areas are flooded for part of the year.

The other condition which appears to be due to the environment in which the ancient Egyptians lived is that of sand pneumoconiosis. Here, as we have seen, the disease is due to inhalation of fine sand particles during sand-storms. It would appear, therefore, that the ancient Egyptians were in danger of contracting disease, both during the period of the year when water was plentiful due to the inundation, as well as when the land was dry and sand-storms occurred.

The electron microscope

The use of the electron microscope is now well established and has been used in many scientific investigations, but its application to the study of Egyptian mummies has been neglected until recently, even though electron microscopes have been readily available to research establishments since the 1950s. The electron microscope was used in this study not only to augment the results obtained by other methods, but also to determine what remained identifiable of the micro-structure of

A modern electron microscope – the AEI *Corinth 500*

the mummified tissues and to show how good the embalmers were at preserving bodies. Specialized electron microscopes were used to determine more fully the nature of various diseases in Egyptian society, to identify the chemicals used in the embalming process, and to examine many of the dead insects which have been found in the mummies.

It would, perhaps, be helpful at this stage to give a brief explanation of the electron microscope and the way in which specimens have to be prepared for examination. The electron microscope does not just magnify specimens many thousands of times, as this in itself would yield little if any more information than a conventional light microscope. The real significance of the electron microscope lies in its ability to show much more detail in a specimen. This increase in information content, or resolving power, is a result of the wavelength of the radiation which is used to illuminate the specimen. In essence, this means that an electron microscope can show up details in a specimen approximately one thousand times smaller than would be possible in a normal light microscope. To achieve this fantastic performance electron microscopes have to be precision-built, and hence they are extremely expensive. The microscope itself is a bulky instrument comprising pumps, electronics, dials, switches, and a camera (see page 137). Operating the microscope is relatively simple, but specimen preparation requires more technical skill.

Egyptian mummies are dry and leather-like, sometimes brittle. Small pieces of tissue from the mummies, or pieces from the dried remains of body organs found in the associated canopic jars, have to be prepared in a fairly elaborate way before they can be examined in the electron microscope. The pieces of tissue selected for examination should be small, preferably less than one millimetre in diameter. They are then rehydrated and 'fixed' using methods similar to those for conventional histology (see pages 130-1). However, the tissue is not embedded in paraffin wax but in a hard plastic. This plastic permeates the whole specimen and is necessary to support the very thin slices of tissue through which the electron beam passes to produce an image. These thin slices of tissue, less than a thousandth of a millimetre thick, are produced on a special instrument called an ultramicrotome. Such ultra-thin sections cannot be produced by the kind of steel knives used in histology, and so the edge of accurately broken glass is often used, as this is much sharper. Unfortunately, many of the mummy samples contain hard particles which very rapidly blunt even the sharpest glass edges, and in these cases very expensive diamond blades have to be used as they have an edge which is much more durable. Thin slices of mummy tissue, if

examined without further treatment, would reveal very little detail. This problem is common to all biological specimens and is overcome by staining various components of the tissue with selected chemicals. After staining, the specimens are ready for examination in the electron microscope, and if an interesting or unusual feature is observed it can be permanently recorded by taking a photograph with the camera which is built into the microscope.

The mummy tissues examined by the electron microscope show a wide range of preservation. Some, such as heart muscle, skeletal muscle, and liver tissue, are generally well preserved, with certain cell components being easily recognizable. A comparison of normal and mummified muscle shows that the characteristic striations are still present. These striations are an expression of the molecular structure of the muscle, which allows its fibres to elongate or contract as the muscle performs its normal function of moving the various parts of the body. Electron microscopy of some liver from a canopic jar has proved most rewarding. This soft organ is very susceptible to putre-faction if it is not removed and dried soon after death, and it was, therefore, something of a surprise when liver cells were readily observable under the electron microscope. Within some of these cells the nucleus was readily identified. This was particularly interesting in view of the difficulty of staining cell nuclei in conventional histology. The membranes bounding the cells were clearly delineated and displayed small areas known as desmosomes, where adjacent cell membranes are in intimate contact and where cell-to-cell communication is thought to occur. Probably the most fascinating find of all was the identification of tiny structures known as centrioles within the cells of this liver. In life, these tiny structures control the division of the cell nucleus prior to cell division. Cell division is an important process, which allows organs to repair damage and to replace old cells. There was, in addition, some evidence of liver-fluke infection since pieces of the liver from one area contained the remains of a fluke-like animal, but exact indenti-fication of this fluke has not been possible. Liver-flukes cause inflammation and fibrosis in the liver when established there, but there was no evidence of fibrosis in the conventional histological sections of the liver in this case although it is probable that the infestation was at an early stage and that clinical symptoms were not present in life.

Other mummified tissues examined under the electron microscope proved somewhat disappointing, as their general structural preservation proved to be poor. This was particularly so in the case of the brain. Examination of pieces of brain from

One of the canopic jars containing the mummified viscera of Nekht Ankh from which the lung tissue was rehydrated and examined

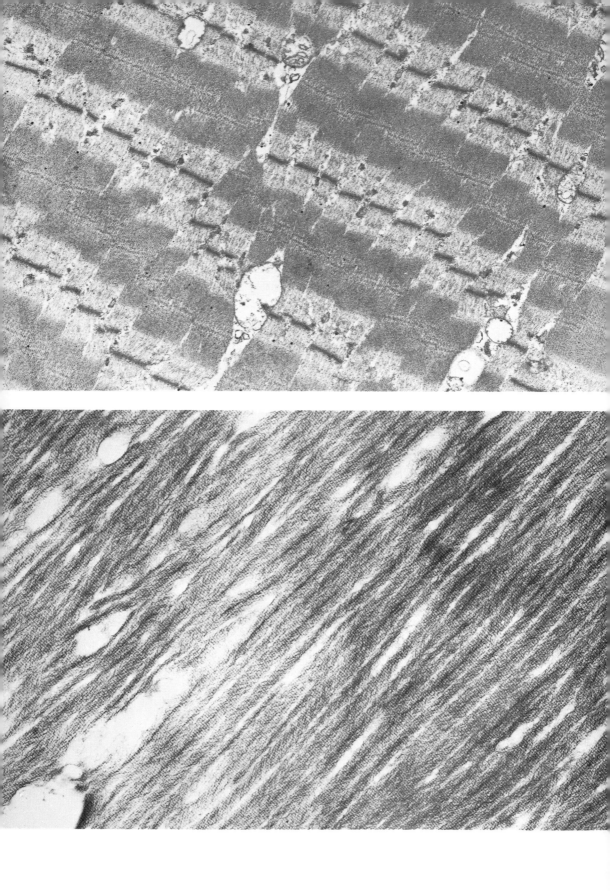

the collection yielded a plentiful supply of bacteria and fungi, which must have grown in the brain substance. The lack of preservation in some brain tissue left behind within the skull in one mummy indicated that considerable putrefaction had occurred before the brain was removed, via the nose, and the body packed with natron. This observation of putrefaction is in keeping with the suggestion of other researchers that the brain was allowed to putrefy and become partially liquified in order to facilitate removal.

Despite the relatively poor preservation of other organs, the electron microscope has contributed significantly to the elucidation of two problems which arose during the histological examination of the intestines of Asru and the lungs of Nekht Ankh. It was mentioned earlier that worms were found in the lining and wall of the intestines of Asru. Electron microscopy of the worms gave more information of their structure and this in turn gave clues as to their origin. The observation of various structures indicated that the worms were nematodes, or round worms, and a subsequent examination of photographs by P. Gooch and other members of the Commonwealth Institute of Helminthology, confirmed this and it was suggested that they were probably of a genus known as *Strongyloides*.

The optical examination of the lungs of Nekht Ankh was also referred to earlier. When this was subjected to examination by electron microscope it showed the accumulation of collagen (fibrous tissue) and elastic tissue round the particles. An analytical electron microscope was used to produce information on the constituents of these tissues. This highly-specialized electron microscope is one of the latest developments of this important instrument and was made available through the kindness of AEI Scientific Apparatus Ltd. All electron microscopes have to be surrounded by lead shields so that harmful x-rays produced by the action of the electrons on the specimen do not escape. In the analytical electron microscope some of these x-rays are collected, and as the type of x-ray emitted is dependent on the constituent producing them we then have the basis of the analysis. The collected x-ray information is processed in a small computer attached to the microscope and the information displayed on a television screen. The crystals in the lung tissue were analysed by this method and were found to contain a large amount of silica, together with some iron, which suggested strongly that they were sand particles.

Present-day disorders caused by lead or mercury poisoning are particularly unpleasant and receive much publicity. In most cases, this poisoning is the result of the inadequate disposal of industrial waste, but we are all exposed to limited quantities of

A comparison of normal human muscle (opposite top) with mummified muscle (below).
The striations running from top right to bottom left in the normal human muscle can be seen to have changed completely in the mummified example. The top picture is magnified 11,200 times and the lower 18,900 times

Sections of mummified liver (top) – magnified 4,800 times – and normal liver (below) – magnified 6,250 times – which show cells with differing nuclei

certain heavy metals in our everyday life. These problems are often regarded as being of fairly recent origin, but one can ask whether ancient civilizations suffered from similar cases of lead or mercury poisoning and, if so, what were the quantities of these metals in the bodies of the ancient Egyptians? The analytical electron microscope allows us to determine whether significant quantities of these harmful elements existed in ancient mummified bodies. Pieces of mummified tissue from three mummies in the Museum collection were analysed with reference to the presence or absence of any heavy metal. This extremely sensitive instrument could not detect any significant trace of these harmful metals in any of the mummies examined. This does not, of course, mean that conditions caused by toxic metals did not occur in ancient Egypt, but is evidence that such conditions were not common in the Egyptian population. These results also permit a comparison of present-day levels of heavy metal accumulation with those of the past, a useful indicator of present-day pollution.

One of the team examining the Manchester mummy collection, Dr Leach, discovered crystalline deposits in the bandages of the mummy 1770. The analytical electron microscope was used to try and elucidate the chemical composition of these deposits. They turned out to be a mixture of salts comprised of sodium, magnesium, sulphur, chlorine, potassium, calcium, iron, and possibly other elements of a lower atomic weight. These elements probably represent the remains of the salt used in the embalming process. In ancient times, before wrapping, the whole body was immersed in natron for up to seventy days and the analytical electron microscope has thus given us more information on the nature of the constituents of the embalmers' dehydrating materials.

A third electron optical method has been used in the study of the mummies. This, the scanning electron microscope, is an instrument which allows us to view the surface of various specimens. Again the advantage of this microscope over a conventional light microscope lies in the ability to discern greater detail. It also has the advantage that much more of the specimen is in focus at the same time. This particular electron microscope produces very detailed, ultra-sharp images on a television screen. For this type of microscope a different method of specimen preparation is required. The specimens have first to be dried, which in the case of mummified tissue is already an accomplished fact. The dried specimens have then to be coated in a precious metal, like gold, so that the electron beam can be reflected off the specimen into a special collector prior to display. The gold coating is sprayed on to the specimen by

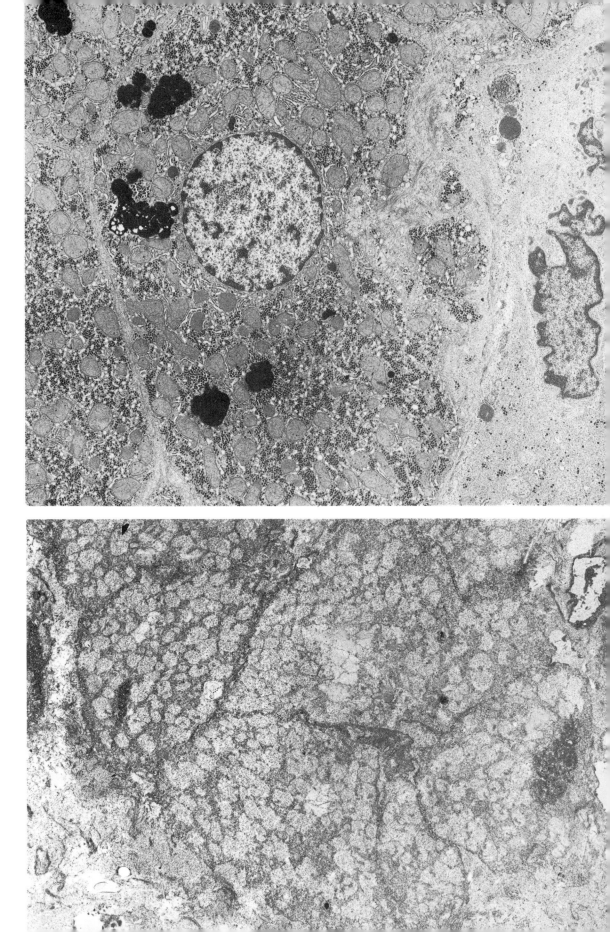

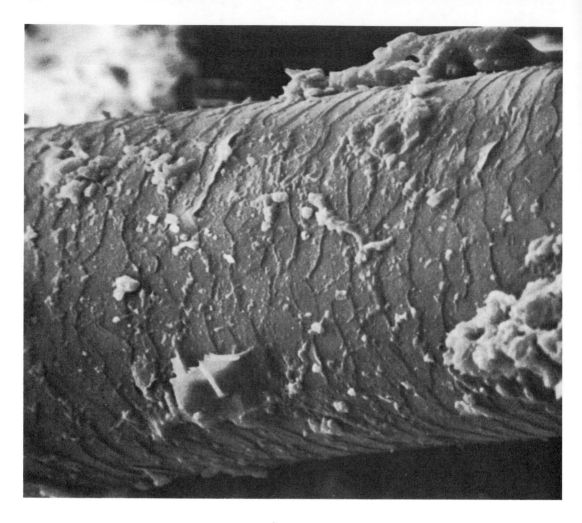

A scanning electron micrograph of human hair from one of the Two Brothers. Magnified 1000 times

vaporizing the metal under vacuum. This method has been used mainly to examine the many insects found in the Manchester mummy collection, but other specimens have been examined. The insects and other animals are described more fully in chapter VIII.

The various electron optical methods have been used to a great extent so that some of the mysteries surrounding the ancient Egyptian civilization could be more fully understood. The method of preparation of Egyptian dead is obviously of great interest. The results obtained indicate that, in the main, the Egyptian embalmers were highly successful in their aim of preserving the earthly form of bodies which they believed would be needed in the after-life. The Egyptian mummies in Manchester Museum, and mummies in other collections throughout the world, are important objects which, if subjected to the many tests now available to modern science, can reveal a tremendous amount of information about diseases in the ancient world, about methods of embalming, and about culture and religion. The advantage of electron microscopy in these investigations is that these precious remains of the ancient world remain relatively intact, as the specimens required by this technique are of such a small size. Future generations will be able to marvel at the Egyptian accomplishments and apply as yet experimental or unknown techniques to more fully understand this and other civilizations, which even with present-day scientific methods, such as electron microscopy, still retain much of their mystery.

In general terms, we were able to determine evidence of diseases in some of the mummies in the collection. Nekht Ankh suffered from sand pneumoconiosis, and pericarditis and pleurisy, which probably resulted from an attack of pneumonia. Asru was affected by a worm infestation of the intestines which was probably caused by a nematode worm of the genus known as *Strongyloides*. In 1770 the remains of a Guinea worm have been found in the anterior abdominal wall. These diseases were closely linked with the Egyptian environment – the sand-storms and large areas of flooded land. Electron microscopy – a relatively new technique in this field of research – provided the additional advantage of discerning greater detail and contributed significantly to the identification of the diseases found in Nekht Ankh and Asru. It also provided additional information on the embalmer's methods of work, on his dehydrating materials, and on the ultimate success of his process.

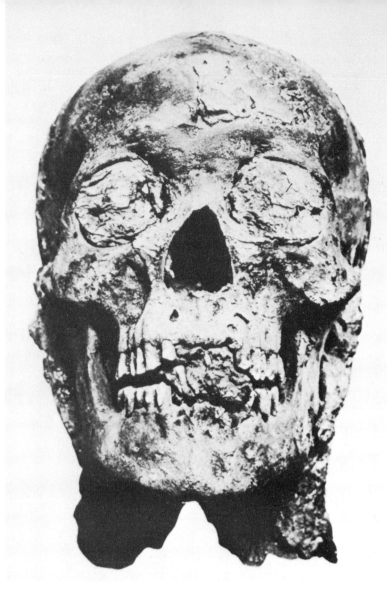

Right: A frontal view of
the head of Pharaoh
Amenophis III, showing
the severely worn teeth
and poor dental condition
Below: A dental chart
showing the main terms
used in the text

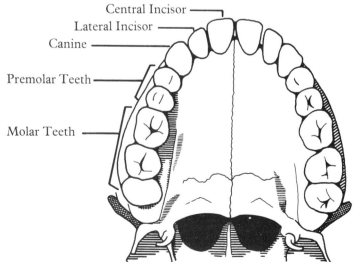

Central Incisor

Lateral Incisor

Canine

Premolar Teeth

Molar Teeth

7 Dental Health and Disease

ONE WOULD GET A TOTALLY MISLEADING IMPRESSION of the dental health of the ancient Egyptians if this was derived solely from teeth visible in the mummies and dry skulls exhibited in museums. Whilst careful examination could possibly reveal certain anomalies, such as a missing tooth or some wear on the biting surface of the teeth, the impression gained would be that of perfectly calcified teeth placed in well-developed arches. It is true that, almost without exception, the calcification of the teeth is excellent, and in this the ancient Egyptians are to be envied, for they were born with teeth not susceptible to decay. Alas, after the early stages of their lives had passed the story is less happy, so much so that for many the effect of bad teeth must have provided problems that were harassing, vexatious, and throughout much of their lives at times extremely painful.

The true picture of the dental health of these people began to emerge when Dr F. Wood-Jones, later to become the first Professor of Human and Comparative Anatomy at the Royal College of Surgeons, went to Egypt in 1907 to assist in the study of human skeletal material from excavations in Nubia. His findings were published in a scholarly treatise and in consequence did not become widely known. It was not until Elliot Smith, the Australian anatomist and anthropologist, published the results of his examination of the royal mummies in the Cairo Museum that the sad plight and dental sufferings of these ancient peoples became more generally known. He found that the condition of the teeth and their supporting structures in many of the royal mummies showed a wide variety of pathological abnormalities. In many cases this was accepted as a natural concomitant of age. It was, however, his description of the dentition of Amenophis III that aroused great astonishment. Worn teeth, abscesses, and the results of chronic and acute gingival inflammation were all to be seen in the mouth of a pharaoh. Any of these conditions would have caused considerable discomfort, as well as intermittent and acute pain and even periods of ill-health. It had always been thought that while the Egyptian peasants would be accustomed to a coarse and consequently tooth-destructive diet, surely that of a pharaoh would be of a much more refined nature.

Ascertaining details of all the dental abnormalities (pathological and non-pathological) of linen-wrapped and even unwrapped mummies gives rise to many problems. In the first place, as the result of mummification and the passage of time, the soft tissues of the face (the skin and the underlying muscles) assume a tough, leather-like, and often brittle consistency, thereby making it quite impossible to open the mouth without irreparable and lasting damage. The result is that no radiographs can be taken inside the mouth. The only projections that can be used (at least when employing a portable or conventional x-ray machine), produce a picture where tissues are superimposed upon one another, causing much of the detail to be obliterated. However, specialized radiological equipment has been developed in the past few years which enables panoramic views of the upper and lower jaws and the teeth to be obtained, and it is often used in orthodontic studies. Some of the Manchester mummy heads were x-rayed by this method, which gave ideal results, although the positioning of a head without a supporting body raised some interesting problems.

A method specially developed for x-raying the teeth of Tutankhamun during the 1968 examination was the use of the radio-active isotope 'Iodine[125]' as the source of energy. This technique produced a vivid picture of the teeth and their surrounding tissues, but it has two disadvantages: first, the isotope must be positioned with great exactitude, impossible to accomplish in a wrapped mummy; and second, the exposure is prolonged. For unwrapped mummies, when conventional radiology is not practical, the technique is ideal.

It is indeed fortunate that we do not have to rely on mummies to give us a complete picture of the dental history of the ancient Egyptians. In various museums and universities in Cairo, Cambridge, Copenhagen, London, Paris, Turin, and other centres, there are extensive collections of dry skulls and these can be studied and, should the abnormality demand it, the skull can be positioned with comparative ease and recorded radiographically. As some of the collections are numbered in hundreds, their study can provide comprehensive and even at times statistical information. It is the study of these skulls, with all their multifarious abnormalities, that has led to a better understanding of the abnormalities to be found in the Manchester collection.

Dental abnormalities are either of a genetic or inherited origin

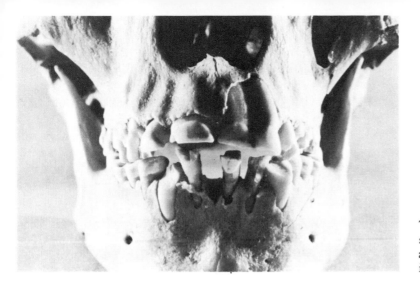

The jaw of Khnum-Nakht
showing the rare
abnormality of two
incisors fused together

or else they are acquired later during life. Almost none in the
genetic class, apart from the possible exception of a cleft palate,
can be described as debilitating. That, however, cannot always
be said of those which develop as life progresses. While some of
these may have no serious or permanent consequences, others
can be responsible for the most profound constitutional
changes.

Possibly the most common non-pathological abnormality
encountered is that of teeth missing from the dentition. Lateral
incisors and premolar teeth sometimes do not develop but as in
modern times, the most common one to fail to develop is the
third molar or wisdom tooth.

An inspection of the teeth in the skull of Khnum Nakht (one
of the Two Brothers) reveals an extremely rare developmental
abnormality. The two central teeth are abnormally large, so
much so that one author has written that they must have given a
most frightening appearance to the face. The left one is even
larger than the right and, surprisingly, has two roots. One
suggestion is that the central and incisor tooth buds fused
together during development and that the next tooth is a super-
numerary or extra one. The other suggestion is that the
abnormal development that took place in both tooth germs was
so great in the case of the left one that it required two roots to
convey its nutrients and that the next tooth was the normal
lateral incisor, which had been displaced because of the lack of
space in the arch.

Of acquired dental disease, that of caries or dental decay is the
one most frequently encountered today but during the pharaonic
period, the results of this scourge were, fortunately, uncommon.
The teeth of the Two Brothers, Nekht Ankh and Khnum Nakht,
who lived during Dynasty XII, are both free of caries and help to
confirm this statement. It is true that pit cavities are sometimes

151

to be seen and occasionally cavities initiated by the fracture of a thin, fragile piece of enamel covering. Rarely, however, does the decay become as rampant as it does in untreated cases today. This freedom from caries, however, does not hold for the people living in the latter periods of Egyptian history, in Graeco-Roman times. It is widely encountered in this period and the Manchester Museum examples are no exception. It is clear from recipes used in cooking during the Roman period that many of the popular dishes were of soft, sticky ingredients and completely lacking in self-cleaning properties. There can be little doubt that it was the change in eating habits that led to this unfortunate change in the resistance of teeth to decay.

From time to time, statements are made suggesting that the teeth of the ancient Egyptians had been treated surgically, but it must be stated categorically that no example has ever been reported by a palaeopathologist, and the authenticity of such a statement must be treated with the utmost suspicion unless vouched for by an accepted authority on the subject.

Had any mummy other than 1770 been made available to the investigating team, the opening of this paragraph would have been written in even more emphatic terms. Even so, it is still true to say that the abnormality that distinguishes ancient Egyptian teeth from those of earlier or later peoples is the excessive attrition (the wear on the biting surface of the teeth), to be seen in almost every example. Peculiarly, the teeth of 1770 show no sign of wear whatsoever, and a suggestion why this individual does not conform to the general pattern will be discussed later. The amount of attrition varies from skull to skull, but examination shows that the extent is usually in direct ratio to the age of the individual at death. It is true that the teeth of earlier populations of this and other countries all exhibit attrition. There cannot be any doubt that the coarse and unrefined diet of those days, including bread made from grain imperfectly cleaned and ground on querns made of soft stones, is the responsible factor in all these cases. Comparative investigations, however, show that the attrition on the teeth of the peoples of ancient Egypt is exceptional. The wear planes on the tooth surface are most complex; they are never, as might be expected, worn down horizontally. In one example a tooth is deeply worn on the cheek side while on the side adjacent to the tongue it is hardly denuded at all. In another, the reverse is true, and in a third example the surface is deeply hollowed out. To complicate the picture, the wear pattern is rarely the same on both front and back teeth.

Although the cause of attrition is not the subject of this chapter, it is so vital to the study of the dental abnormalities in

A wooden model of servants preparing bread. This shows them grinding corn, making and shaping the dough, and preparing loaves for baking

ancient Egyptian human remains that it is worthwhile digressing a little. The general range of food eaten by the ancient Egyptians is well documented. Paintings on the tomb walls show the slaughtering of animals, the catching of wild duck, and the growing and harvesting of grain. There are also inscriptions on the walls of temples revealing the amounts of food carried by armed expeditions, and the particulars of plunder brought back following a victorious campaign. There is even the more tangible evidence: quantities of various foods and fruits placed in the tomb for use by the deceased during life in the after world. A surprising feature is the size of the daily ration of bread to Egyptian troops; that it was large is confirmed by the fact that the Greeks had a nickname for the contemporary Egyptians, 'artophagi' (eaters of bread), and it is bread that appears to have been the chief source of trouble.

During 1971 an exhibition in Manchester Museum displayed a large number of pieces of ancient Egyptian bread. These had been x-rayed and the vast amount of mineral fragments in each piece came as a considerable surprise. The minerals were identified, and while some came from the soil in which the grain had been grown, and some from the grinding stones, by far the largest proportion was pure quartz. It then became obvious that the dominant factor was wind-blown desert sand, which (one can say with hindsight) should have been expected. During certain seasons of the year dust-storms are, and always have been, a part

A good example of how the food of ancient Egypt could wear down the upper teeth.
In this case secondary dentine has formed fast enough to prevent the otherwise inevitable development of disease

of Egyptian life, and no particular stretch of imagination is required to picture the great contamination of grain by wind-blown sand during harvesting, winnowing, and storage. A certain percentage of mineral fragments could, however, have been a deliberate addition. Pliny and other ancient writers refer to the custom of the Carthaginians of first pounding the grain with a pestle and then adding bricks, chalk, and sand, prior to grinding the grain. The necessity for such a procedure was recently confirmed by Dr John Prag of Manchester Museum. Using ancient grinding stones he found that after grinding the corn for fifteen minutes the grains remained unchanged. When, however, a percentage of sand was added to the sample, fine flour rapidly resulted. Those who have eaten sandwiches on a sandy, wind-swept beach can have nothing but compassion and sympathy for the ancient Egyptians, who would have eaten similarly contaminated bread on every occasion, with dire consequences to their teeth, and consequently to their well-being.

The picture of dental attrition has already been stressed, but for many individuals that is only the beginning of a melancholy story. In many cases this progressed until the pulp chamber iself was exposed. This houses the nerve and blood supply to the tooth. Fortunately, in many cases, because of a reaction to the irritation set up by the abrasive processes, the cells of the dental pulp laid down a protective barrier of secondary dentine. In favourable cases this progressed faster than the wear, so forming a protective barrier against any invading organisms. In those cases where this reaction failed to keep pace with the wear, the pulp chamber became exposed and disease-generating bacteria were able to invade the tissues; inflammation resulted, to be followed in due course by putrefaction. Unfortunately, the sequence did not end there, as these same organisms proceeded to invade the surrounding tissues and, according to the inborn resistance of the individual, produced chronic or acute abscesses, fistulae, or cysts. In many cases that is as far as the sequence extended. In a number of instances, however, possibly aided by an unfortunate choice of remedy, an infection of the upper jaw would follow, which in most cases would curtail the expectancy of life. In even more unfortunate examples, an acute abscess would invade the neck which, even in these days of advanced surgical and chemical therapy, can end in death.

There are other afflicting results from severe and irregular attrition. Because of over-closure of the lower jaw (due to the reduced height of the teeth), changes took place in the mandibular joint which could give rise to arthritic pains and also to possible dislocation of the lower jaw. It is known that this was a factor in daily life in ancient times, as the condition is fully described in the Smith Surgical Papyrus. This is a medical treatise written during the New Kingdom (1552-1069 BC) and Breasted's translation of one of the text reads:

If thou examinest a man having a dislocation in his mandible, shouldst thou find his mouth open (and) cannot close for him, thou shouldst put thy thumb(s) upon the two ends of the rami of the mandible in the inside of his mouth, (and) thy two claws (meaning two groups of fingers) under his chin (and) thou shouldst cause them to fall back so they rest in their place.

The dislocation of the jaw to be seen in the head of mummy 7740 cannot, however, be attributed to such a cause. It shows no signs of abnormality and the dislocation is almost certainly the result of injury. For how long one could survive in such a state, assuming there were no other injuries of a fatal nature, depends upon the circumstances of daily life. Nourishment could be sucked in through a tube, but active enjoyment would certainly be hindered. As well as suffering from a dislocated jaw, 7740 had about ten badly decayed teeth, most of which had abscesses beneath them; he had also lost three front teeth because of an infection of the surrounding bone, so his daily pleasure in life must have been marred for a very long time.

It is said that in this country more teeth are lost annually from pyorrhea than from any other cause. Pyorrhea is essentially an infection of the tooth-supporting structures and usually starts from without and progresses inwards. The same term could be applied to a condition frequently seen in mouths of the ancient Egyptians, but the cause in most cases was very different. It was due to the tissues that support the teeth not being able to withstand the pressures of the heavy loads of mastication. These pressures increased greatly as the teeth were worn down and changed in shape. The bone in the upper jaw is not so compact as the lower and consequently not so strong, and in many instances, as in mummy 1976/51A, all the upper teeth are missing and the palate completely flat, while many of the lower teeth are still present, albeit decayed and much worn.

The age range of the human remains in the Manchester Museum collection varies from two years to advanced adult life, and their dental histories have been covered by one or more of the themes discussed in this chapter. Two specimens, however, warrant further study, in so far as details of the death of one, and inferences on the general health of the other, can be deduced.

An inspection of the x-ray showing the front teeth of the head of mummy 22940 shows that the incisor teeth are fractured. There is really nothing unusual in this as so much post-mortem

Opposite above:
The cleaned facial bones
of mummy 1770
Opposite below:
As part of the facial
reconstruction of 1770
a plaster skull was made
from the many fragments
which remained. Pegs
were then inserted to
indicate the depth of the
soft tissue at each point

damage is done to mummies (from the time they are removed from their initial internment until they are seen in the cases of a museum), that without careful reading of the radiograph this damage could be dismissed as the result of inevitable manhandling. But looking at the root of each tooth, it can be seen that the periodontal membrane (the thin elastic membrane which surrounds the root of the tooth and joins it to the surrounding bone), is thickened. From this we know that the injury took place during lifetime, and it is possible to deduce further that, because the fractured pieces are still *in situ*, consciousness was not regained after the injury. Inspection of the head shows that the lip is extremely swollen and gives the face an unseemly appearance. The apparent head injuries in themselves were not sufficient to cause death, but they were undoubtedly received at the same time as those which proved fatal and life must have ended shortly afterwards.

A mummy more unpromising from the dental point of view than 1770 could not possibly have been produced for the investigating team. The revealing x-ray pictures that had been taken prior to unwrapping showed that the mummy was extremely youthful, and would provide no abnormalities in the teeth, and certainly no pathological ones on which to report. And eventually, when the facial bones were first removed from the wrappings, covered with debris, a less helpful or inspiring sight could not possibly be imagined. How wrong first impressions can be! First, by the state of the eruption of the teeth the age was established. The third molar teeth were present, but unerupted, and the radiograph showed the development of the roots of the second molars, so that the age at death could be fixed as being between thirteen and fourteen years. Then, after seeing that the normal number of teeth were present, an astonishing fact was observed: namely, that the cusps of the teeth were unblemished and quite free from wear. This was most surprising, because it is rare to see even deciduous molar teeth without some flattening of the cusps. Close examination revealed a number of other interesting features. In the upper jaw there were two irregularly placed teeth with a triangular space between, near to the gum margin. Such a space is a persistent trap for food particles and there is usually considerable difficulty in removing strands of fibrous food from it. This results in a chronic infection of the gum and the production of a bony crater in the underlying bone. None of these signs was present, which suggests that her diet was a soft one, probably more liquid than solid, or that she swallowed her food without any attempt to masticate it efficiently. In either case it argues against a robust or healthy constitution.

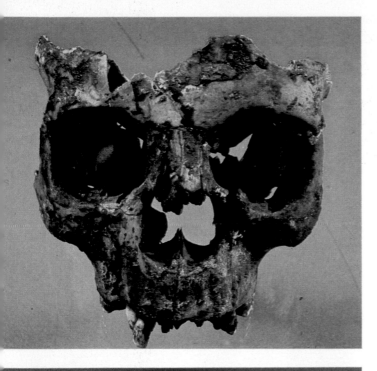

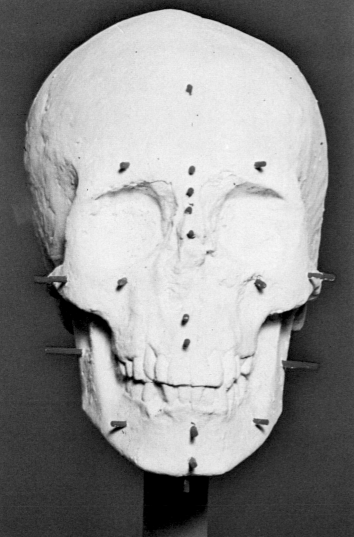

Knowing that the thin bones forming the interior part of the nose are extremely fragile and easily broken when a mummy is first unwrapped, a detailed inspection was made as soon as the overlying debris was removed. It was observed that what remained of the nasal septum was seriously deflected and the turbinate bones were also much enlarged and deflected, so much so that during life, when covered with mucous membrane (which, in these circumstances, would also be swollen and congested), nasal breathing would be practically impossible. That she did, in fact, breathe mainly through her mouth is confirmed by the pitting to be seen on the alveolar bone margin surrounding the upper front teeth. This would result from a chronic inflammation of the gingival tissues, which is the outcome of continuous mouth breathing. In all probability she inherited a short upper lip pattern, as this seems to be frequently associated with nasal congestion. That she did not succumb to the habit of thumb-sucking is indicated by the fact that her upper incisor teeth did not protrude; a short upper lip combined with thumb-sucking invariably results in protruding front teeth. It is interesting to note that there are a number of Old Kingdom statuettes showing families with the younger members so consoling themselves.

One other piece of information emerged from an examination of the facial bones, the fact that her face was asymmetrical or lop-sided; the canine fossa on the left side was so much depressed that it would have distorted the harmony of the facial features.

It would be out of place in this general discussion on the dental health of the ancient Egyptians to give a detailed resumé of each dentition in the collection. It is sufficient to record that the examination revealed a wide variety of abnormalities, both pathological and non-pathological. All the evidence obtained supports the widely held belief that of those of the population who died in childhood and during the adolescent period, dental disease played no part in their early demise. But for those in mature and older age groups (unless magic spells produced more favourable results than they would today) the ills engendered by their dental ailments would have promoted, in varying degrees, discomfort, pain, inability to masticate food effectively, constitutional disturbances, and in a number of cases would even have hastened death itself.

The body coffins of the Two Brothers which contained the mummies investigated in 1906

159

8 The Fauna

THE STUDY OF THE MANY small invertebrate animals found with the Manchester mummies was an opportunity to gain an insight into some aspects of Egyptian life. Did the ancient Egyptians suffer from the same parasites as modern man and did they have to tolerate the same household insect pests? Unlike many other civilizations in the ancient world, the Egyptians stored food as a safeguard against famine, and they also effectively stored their dead. Insects have been found in storage jars from tombs and also in canopic jars containing mummified viscera, thus one might suppose that insect pests were a problem.

The finding of dead insects with mummies does not necessarily mean that the infestation originated in antiquity. The parasitic worms found in this examination of the Manchester mummies must have been present in ancient times as these parasites need living hosts. Insects, however, which are by far the most numerous species of any animal group known to man and possibly the one with the greatest diversity of habitat, are not so easily placed as regards time of infestation. Depending on their habits, beetles could invade mummies either at the time of death, during embalming, in the tomb, during transportation, or even on display in a museum. Beetles are easily recognized as the adults possess a pair of hard, shiny wing coverings (elytra) which meet neatly along the mid-line of the dorsal surface of the abdomen. A small number of these can be serious pests in museum collections if special precautions are not taken. The museum beetle *Anthrenus museorum* is a cosmopolitan species and has been found in Egyptian remains recently collected in Egypt but not in any of the Manchester mummies. It is somewhat easier to deduce the time of infestation by flies since their larval stages require a moist food source. The true flies or *Diptera* differ from other insects by the presence on the adult body of a single pair of membranous wings. Adult flies probably lay eggs on a body at the time of death. But even here there may be uncertainty, as some dipteran flies can infect the human body

Insects found
in mummy 1770.
Top left: *Necrobia rufipes*.
Top right: puparia of the common house fly, *musca domestica*.
Bottom left: the wing case of a carabid beetle.
Bottom right: puparia of the cheese skipper, *Piophila casei*

during life and cause a type of disease called myiasis. Myiasis is the infestation of living human or vertebrate animals with dipterous larvae, which feed on the tissues of the hosts. Such infections are particularly unpleasant but fortunately few myiasis-producing flies attack humans. The basic problem of identifying at which point infection occurred can be tackled by knowing the habits of the insects concerned and also their life histories.

Insects usually leave remains, some of which are relatively easy to identify. In life, the soft internal parts are protected by an external skeleton which is resilient, impervious to water, and does not rot on the death of the insect, unlike the bodies of other soft-bodied creatures. Insects belong to a group of animals called arthropods or literally 'jointed-limbs'. If joints were not present in the limbs, head, and body to facilitate movement, the skeleton would be completely restrictive. Muscles are attached to the inside of the exo-skeleton (the external skeleton), near joints, to facilitate movement. The joints are flexible extensions of the hard exo-skeleton and are also impermeable to water loss. Water loss to small creatures is probably their most serious problem. Being small they have a large surface area relative to their volume. If the exo-skeleton were not waterproof, moisture would rapidly escape through this surface and harm the creature. Insects have been successful in overcoming this problem and this fact is probably the major reason for their abundance on this planet and their ability to adapt to so many different habitats. The external skeleton, which in life is so essential to the insect, leaves an identifiable shell on death. Most insects are identified by the various features found on the exo-skeleton and in the case of adult insects this can be done relatively easily. Immature stages of insects are less simply identified. Insects have a complex life-cycle in which they change form several times. The life histories of the two major groups of insects found on the mummies can be summarized as follows. An adult insect lays eggs which hatch out into larvae on or near the body. As the larvae eat the body tissues or the bandages, they grow, but the external skin eventually restricts growth and they then moult and replace the old tight skin with a new larger one so that growth can continue. This cycle may be repeated several times until the larvae are large enough to metamorphose into adult insects. The final larval stage becomes quiescent and produces a pupa or puparium in which larval tissues are broken down and reorganized into adult ones. Finally the adult escapes from the pupa, finds a mate and the life-cycle begins again. Because of this complex life-cycle the adult insect and its larvae can exploit different food sources. This means that larvae or adults can be

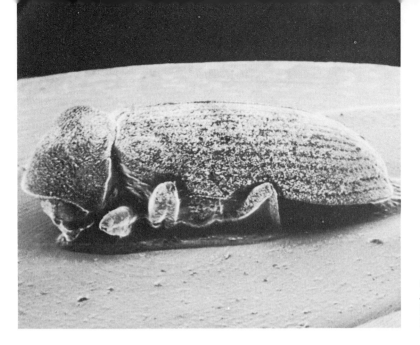

An adult woodworm,
Anobium punctatum, found
in a wooden sarcophagus.
Magnified 26 times

present alone, or both may be present together in a good source, depending on the particular needs of that species.

Adult insects are generally much more mobile than larvae and may crawl or fly away to a new food source. Thus in the case of the flies found in the Manchester mummies, larvae and puparia have been frequently found but only one adult fly. The much more active adults probably left while conditions allowed them to do so. The larval stages of insects are much less well known scientifically than those of adults and hence are more difficult to identify. Often insects from the mummies are incomplete, because parts of their bodies have broken off and are missing, rendering identification difficult. Expert help from two relevant institutions was therefore sought. Mr A. Brindle and Mr C. Johnson at the Manchester Museum's Department of Entomology, and Mr K. Smith at the British Museum (Natural History), willingly identified problematical species, where possible.

Most of the insects found had used the sarcophagus, bandages, or body as a food source. The common woodworm (*Anobium punctatum*) was present in the sarcophagi of several of the mummies and infestation could have occurred at any time.

Mummy 1770, the subject of the unwrapping, contained within its bandages a multitude of insects. The two commonest were a beetle (*Necrobia rufipes*) and a dipteran fly (*Piophila casei*). Adult beetles were present but only one adult fly was found, the majority of the fly's remains being puparia. *Piophila* puparia found in the body cavity of the mummy unwrapped in Detroit were covered in resin from the embalming process. As 1770 was unwrapped, only a small number of puparia were found in the outer bandage layers, whereas the inner bandages contained

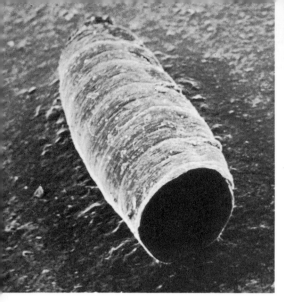 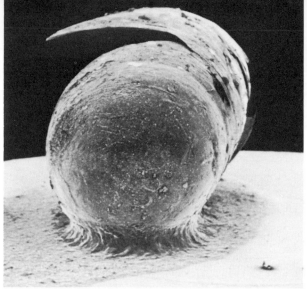

Above left: The empty
puparium of *Piophila casei.*
Magnified 29 times
Above right: The end
view of a house fly
puparium. Magnified
30 times

many. This observation, in conjunction with the Carbon-14
dating results which revealed that the bandages were of a much
more recent origin than the body, suggests that 1770 was at least
partially rehydrated before being rewrappped. Flies need moist
food sources as their larvae cannot ingest dry food. This means
that some of the fly remains found in 1770 may have come from
eggs deposited shortly after death while all those found in the
bandages were deposited on the rehydrated body during
rewrapping hundreds of years later. No puparia of *Piophila*
would have been found in the bandages had the body been
rewrapped without becoming rehydrated. *Piophila* is more
commonly known as the cheese skipper and is a domestic pest. It
is known to breed in cheese, bacon, ham, and similar foodstuffs,
and because of these habits, it can be eaten accidentally. The
larvae are extremely resistant to gastric juices and consequently
can survive to attack the gut wall and cause bleeding of the
intestine. Mummy 1770 may well have been infected during life,
but as *Piophila* is a pest of stored meat, it seems likely that eggs
were laid on the body after death. *Necrobia* (beetle), in addition to
eating some of the flesh of 1770, would probably have attacked
and eaten the larvae of the cheese skipper, as it has been reported
to prey on larvae of other species found in the same food.

A few puparia of the common house fly (*Musca domestica*) were
also found in the remains of 1770. This species is probably the
most familiar of all insects and has accompanied man every-
where. It breeds in waste food or faeces providing the larval food
source is not too dry. Again, this means that either the eggs were
laid before the body dried out completely after death, or that the
body became rehydrated at some period subsequent to the
original embalming, which was perhaps caused by flooding of the
original tomb.

164

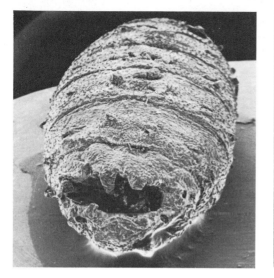 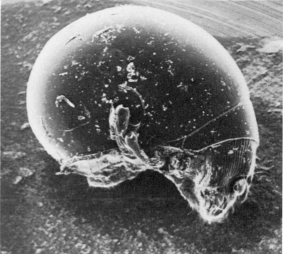

The many insects found in 1770 did not have as idyllic a life as might at first appear, even though surrounded by food, because remains of a carabid beetle were also found. Carabids are predatory beetles and were no doubt feeding on the other insects present in the tissues and wrappings of 1770.

The remains of the Two Brothers, Nekht Ankh and Khnum Nakht, were also inundated with insects, but these differed from those found in 1770. Again the two predominant species were a fly and a beetle. Puparia of a dipteran fly (*Chrysomyia albiceps*) were common and as with the cheese skipper, this fly was also found in a mummy recently unwrapped in Detroit (Pum II). *Chrysomyia* lays eggs on carrion, which the larvae eat voraciously, but it also has predacious and cannabalistic habits. The behaviour of the larvae of *Chrysomyia albiceps* can give rise to secondary myiasis. Wounds infested by larvae of a different fly are attacked by *Chrysomyia*. Here the larvae of *Chrysomyia* prey on the original larvae of the wound, but can also attack the tissues of that wound as well. However, such cases of secondary myiasis have not been reported in man.

Larvae of *Chrysomyia* have also been found in rehydrated tissues of Asru. A piece of stomach was placed in a solution of formalin and after several hours some larval skins of *Chrysomyia* floated out. This method of retrieving insect remains is important as these larvae would have been difficult to find and identify had they remained entombed in the dry stomach.

The predominant beetle in the remains of the Two Brothers was an unusual species. *Gibbium psylloides* is unusual because it resembles a giant mite and has the common name of the hump-spider beetle. This animal is a serious pest of vegetable products and may have used the bandages as a food source. *Gibbium* has long been known to infest grain products and has

Above left: Puparium of *Chrysomyia albiceps*. Magnified 28 times
Above right: An adult hump-spider beetle, *Gibbium psylloides*. Magnified 36 times

165

been reported previously from the tombs of the Egyptian pharaohs. Smaller numbers of a second beetle, *Mesostenopa*, were also found in the remains of the Two Brothers. Some beetles related to *Mesostenopa* are known to be pests of stored food, while others are scavengers in hot, sandy regions.

An object of obvious insect origin was found attached to the wrappings of mummy 1767, another mummy in the Manchester collection, and proved to be an egg-case of the cockroach *Blatta orientalis*. The egg-case was attached firmly to the bandages of this mummy by the wax or resin used during the wrapping of the body, and was thus of ancient origin. The cockroach, like the common house fly, appears to have been associated with man for many thousands of years. Cockroaches attack and consume a wide range of food products and what is not consumed is fouled by a disgusting odour.

Another group of animals has hard coverings which on death leave a permanent record of their existence. These, the molluscs, carry a shell round with them to protect the soft body organs. A snail shell was found in the mud surrounding the limbs of mummy 1770. In its original watery habitat this gastropod snail may have harboured some of the unpleasant helminth diseases thought to be common in ancient Egypt, notably the liver-fluke (*Fasciola hepatica*). The adult is parasitic in a vertebrate host, such as man, while its larval stages are always parasitic in a snail, and so both hosts are necessary for the completion of the life-cycle.

Remains of parasitic worms, or of any soft-bodied creature, are always extremely difficult to identify. Most soft-bodied worms would simply putrefy on death. In this study, the remains of three parasitic worms have been found and in view of their susceptibility to decay this is quite an achievement. They have been found for two quite different reasons, both of which, however, contributed to their preservation. Correctly embalmed body organs were dried in salts, which would also dry and hence preserve the parasites in those organs. Of course, this would happen only if the embalming was done fairly quickly after death. The liver-fluke and nematode worm (*Strongyloides*) were preserved because they became desiccated during embalming. Worms also, on occasion, become calcified by calcium carbonate precipitation in the living host if conditions are suitable. Calcification leaves a permanent fossil record of that creature. The Guinea worm (*Dracunculus medinensis*) found by Professor Isherwood in the radiographs of 1770, was calcified and was only revealed by the x-ray examination.

In contrast, most previous records of parasitic worm infestations have come from analysis of ancient faecal remains (coprolites). The eggs or cysts of most parasitic worms are extremely resistant to decay and are passed out of the intestine in large numbers. Analysis of coprolites can reveal many of these cysts, which can be extremely difficult to identify. No such analysis could have been attempted here and anyway it is more satisfying to find worm remains in human tissues.

Plant remains and seeds have been observed within the wrappings of 1770 by Dr Leach. These may have become incorporated accidentally into the wrappings, or perhaps have been placed there deliberately as part of the burial ritual. Fungal remains, bacteria, and bacterial spores have been found in many mummy tissues. These micro-organisms were, without doubt, responsible for much of the original putrefaction of the body tissues, especially the brain, lungs, and intestine.

The Egyptian art of mummification was to some extent countered by the ravages of the insects, the fungi, and the bacteria. These organisms use the body as a source of food and not as a sacred object. Of the two types of insects commonly encountered, the dipteran flies probably infested the bodies prior to or during embalming. Some of the beetles, though, may have infested the mummies at any time during their history. Thus the common insect pests of man today – the house fly and the cockroach – were probably just as much a problem to the ancient Egyptians in the household, and in food storage buildings, and also a serious nuisance to the embalmer. The finding of parasitic fluke and worm infections supports the theory that such diseases were common in ancient Egypt, making life at times fairly unpleasant for those affected.

The detailed examination of the fauna found in association with the Manchester mummies has added to our knowledge of their daily life. With the aid of the electron microscope, it has been possible to identify some of the parasites from which they suffered. The discovery of three parasitic worms in the mummies was due to a fortunate chance of preservation, since most are susceptible to decay, and most previous records of parasitic worm infestations have come not from human tissues but from the analysis of ancient faecal remains.

Also the examination of insects, which invaded the body and its wrappings after death and used it as a food source, has provided further useful information, particularly in the case of 1770, where the indications are that the body was partially rehydrated before rewrapping.

9 Faces and Fingerprints

THE DISCOVERY AND RECONSTRUCTION of artefacts left by man has always been of prime importance to archaeologists and of great value to historians, for they provide evidence of cultures and ways of life which have long since vanished. Remains of the people who made and used these artefacts are of equal importance, for they provide an opportunity to assess their physical characteristics and to some extent their health. However, they do not tell us anything about the actual appearance of people. It was to this end that a programme of facial reconstruction was undertaken in an attempt to provide a 'bridge' which would enable the dried bones of ancient Egyptians to be seen as living people. The embalmed bodies of the ancient Egyptians provide us with a good deal more information than most other human remains. Indeed, so well has the embalming been done that occasionally the heads and faces appear to have undergone relatively little change. Sadly, though, this is the exception and the body often bears little resemblance to a living person since it is often little more than a skeleton in appearance.

Because of the difficulty in relating dried and skeletal remains to living people, it was decided to make reconstructions of some of the mummies which were of special interest or demonstrated some particular disease. It was recognized that there would be a limit to the authenticity of such reconstructions, but in all cases the highest degree of accuracy was aimed at. The head and face are perhaps the most important and characteristic aspect of any individual, and it was in this area that effort was concentrated. Ultimately, it should be possible to work from radiographs of wrapped subjects, but to date all work has been on unwrapped subjects, and although not from choice, none of those selected had any notable remnants of soft tissue.

The first two mummies chosen are in many ways unique, and had the advantage of having been very closely studied. They were unwrapped by Dr Margaret Murray at Manchester Museum

The final appearance of the head of 1770, reconstructed in wax and fitted with glass eyes, eyelashes, and a wig

in 1906; all her findings were very carefully documented and a considerable amount of work has been done on them since. It is known that they were buried together in the rock-tombs of Der Rifeh, and date from Dynasty XII. From the hieroglyphs on the coffins it appears that they were half-brothers, sharing a common mother, and all the evidence seems to suggest that the younger of the two, Khnum Nakht, had a negro father. He was probably about forty to forty-five when he died, and suffered from osteo-arthritis which had seriously affected his back. He also appears to have had some form of palsy in one foot, and the configuration of two of his front teeth was unusual. The elder brother, Nekht Ankh, died at approximately sixty years of age, and there is speculation that he may have been a eunuch. This much is known from the remains, and the task was now to try and bring them to life.

Although the ultimate aim was to make paintings and drawings, it was decided to do the initial reconstructions three-dimensionally. There are distinct advantages in this method, for example, to serve as models from which paintings and other studies could be made from all angles. Work of this kind has been done before, notably by Kollman and Buchly in Germany who, in 1898, published a paper in which they included a series of tables listing the thickness of soft tissue at twenty-six points on the human face. These measurements included the maximum and minimum thickness in both men and women of various ages. It can, of course, be argued that these scales are not universally applicable, but they are the only scientifically accurate scales available, and most work of this kind has been based on them. Before any reconstruction could be started, casts of the two skulls had to be made. Using techniques for making medical models developed in the University Department of Medical Illustration we first prepared a mould in a flexible compound called algenate. This was achieved by placing the prepared skull on its side in a container and pouring in algenate until half of it was covered. This was allowed to set, then the rest of the skull was covered with a second layer of algenate. When the second layer had set, the entire mould with the now embedded skull was removed from the container. The two halves were then opened up and the skull removed, providing us with a 'split mould' into which plaster-of-paris was introduced. The result was an accurate cast of each skull. Because of the risk of damage, the vulnerable areas were carefully packed before the mould was made. This reduced the complexity of the casting, and although it meant sacrificing some details, it enabled the casts to be made without damaging the original skulls in any way. The lower jaws were treated in a similar way and when complete were fitted to the skulls, which were then mounted on wooden stands.

The next stage was to start building up in modelling clay the soft structures of the face, head, and neck. In the initial stages, the skull very quickly began to take on the recognizable features of a face (p. 173). It must be emphasized at this stage that the work is done as a scientific exercise and does not allow the creator to indulge in artistic licence, but before long, the individual heads began to show distinctive characteristics of their own. This is not surprising as the basic architecture of any face is decided by the underlying bone structure. It was important to make constant reference to the original skull, for although the muscles of the face make no impression on the bone, those of the lower jaw and neck are very distinct and give a good indication of size and strength. When the main shape of the heads had been roughed out they were smoothed down, and accurate measurements were taken to ensure that the thickness conformed with the results established by Kollman and Buchly. When the final modelling was finished and the measurements checked, the results seemed blank and rather expressionless. This must inevitably be the case since we have no evidence of any folds or wrinkles in the skin which are so much a part of any face. In work of this type results are reached by adhering strictly to certain basic rules; to add features for which there is no evidence would be to indulge in pure speculation.

We know that these two men were half-brothers, and the reconstructions seem to confirm the fact, also the negroid appearance of one is quite noticeable. During the process of reconstruction, no reference was made to two small wooden figures found in the coffins. These figures were only about six inches high, but appeared to have specific features. There is unfortunately some confusion over which figure represents which brother, as the names are wrongly inscribed on the statuettes. So beautifully were these figures carved that in spite of the difference in size it was felt that some direct comparisons with the reconstructed heads would be worthwhile, so they were brought to the same size photographically and showed a marked similarity, especially in the case of Nekht Ankh (p. 175).

The pictures of Khnum Nakht are not quite so striking in their similarity but nonetheless both show a broad, powerful head with full lips and a wide nose. Although in no way conclusive, this did show that the work was not entirely speculative. A drawing was made of Khnum Nakht, a few minor adjustments being made, notably round the eyes.

In the case of Nekht Ankh a painting was made with no alterations, showing him with short hair as indicated in the

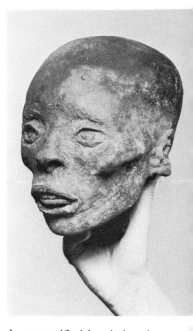

A mummified head showing well-preserved soft tissue. Although the features are very clear, in life the appearance would have been very different.

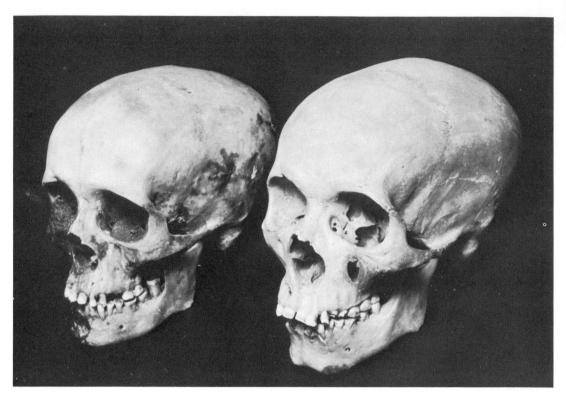

Reconstructing the heads
of the Two Brothers:
Above: The skulls of
the Two Brothers,
Nekht Ankh is on the
left, with Khnum Nakht
on the right.
Right: The skull partly
embedded in algenate to
form the first half
of a mould.
Opposite top: The top
of the algenate mould
removed to show the
plaster cast of the skull.
Below left: The recon-
struction of the face was
built up on the plaster
skull starting with the neck
and base of the skull.
Below right: The partly-
finished model showing
how quickly the skull
takes on a life-like
appearance

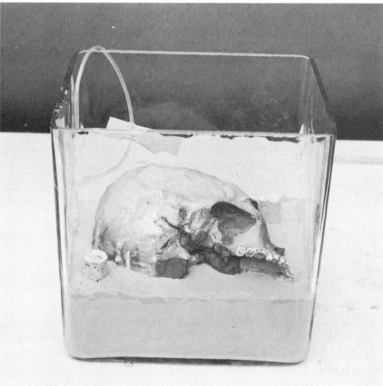

172

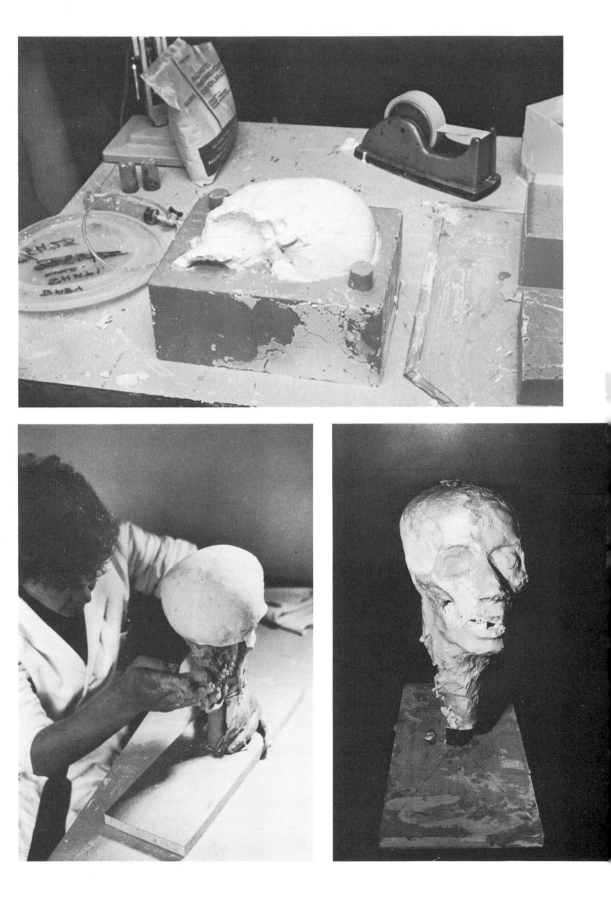

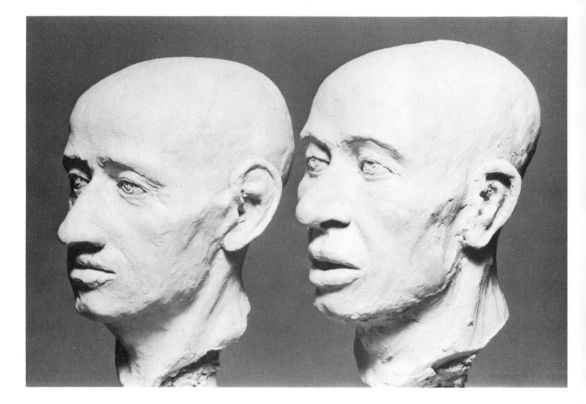

Above: A comparison between the two reconstructions. Nekht Ankh is on the left

Opposite: Two views of the reconstructed head of Nekht Ankh compared with a wooden figurine from his tomb

small carved figure. Any further illustrations that may be made will show him with rather more almond-shaped eyes, a feature of the ancient Egyptians with which we were not familiar at the time of the painting. The reconstruction of the heads of the Two Brothers was relatively straightforward, for both basic skulls were complete, and the background of the two was well documented. This however was not so in the case of the next subject dealt with.

As will be clear from previous chapters, the condition of mummy 1770 was far from perfect, and before unwrapping x-rays had indicated that the skull had been badly damaged. The full extent of the damage became apparent as soon as the wrappings at the neck of the cartonnage mask were removed. The skull had been broken into about thirty separate pieces and lay in a jumbled heap, thickly encrusted with the remains of mud and bandages. Fortunately, the most critical areas had remained undamaged and all the teeth were present. The state of the bones themselves could not be seen until the mud and bandages had been removed, but some of the fragments were very small which made it very difficult to establish their position in the skull of 1770. Before any reconstruction could start there had to be something upon which to work; this meant that the skull would

174

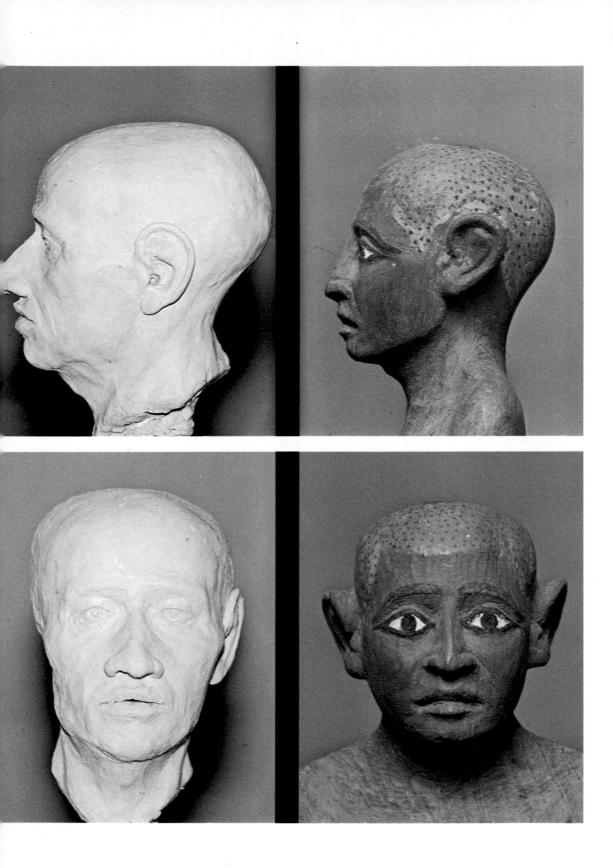

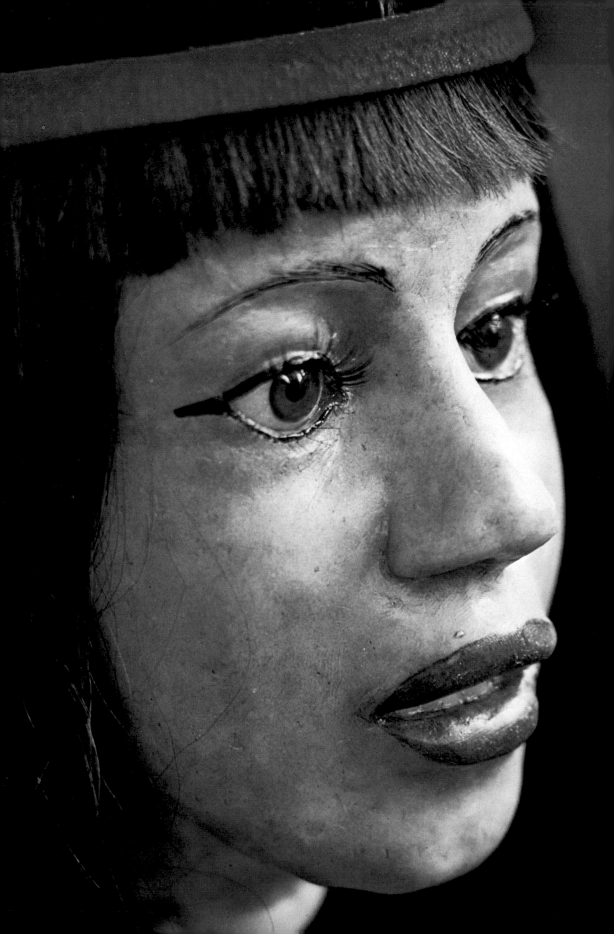

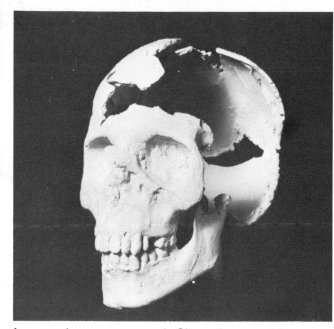 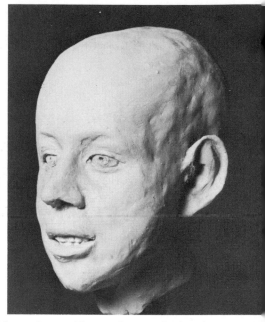

have to be reconstructed. Since the actual bones could not be used, accurate casts in plastic were made of each separate piece; these separate pieces were fitted together, and it was then possible to see how much of the skull was in fact missing. More pieces were absent from the left side than from the right and there is a very obvious defect in the bone in the region of the left-hand side of the nose. The reason for this has not been finally established, but it is reasonable to assume that it must have caused considerable nasal congestion. The next stage was to reconstruct the missing areas to enable a plaster cast to be made. This was done in wax, with little attempt to reproduce fine detail, as it was only the basic shape that was needed. There were a few changes in the methods adopted for the Two Brothers. The lower jaw was cast in position and not as a separate item. Perhaps of greater importance, small pegs were inserted at specific points on the skull, and cut to precise lengths, and these made it considerably easier to build up the soft tissues accurately. The face soon began to take shape, and care was taken to ensure that the features which one associates with young teenagers were taken into account. Because of the assumed nasal congestion the mouth was left slightly open, stressing the adenoidal appearance. At this point the general effect of the head was almost European in appearance. However, after discussions with Dr David and a visit to the British Museum, slight modifications were made to the nose and eyes. These very slight adjustments were sufficient to change the face into a classic example of an ancient Egyptian.

Under normal circumstances, the next step would have been to make drawings, paintings, and photographs of the head. But

Above: the rearticulated skull of 1770 made in plastic. It was now possible to assess the full extent of the missing sections.
Right: The initial clay reconstruction showing all the features in the correct relationship with each other. Modifications were later made to the shape of the eyes, correcting the rather European appearance.

Opposite: A portrait-style shot of the reconstructed head of 1770 which bears a marked resemblance to some modern Egyptians.

177

because of the general popular interest being shown in this mummy, a finished three-dimensional reconstruction was then attempted (p. 176). This model was cast in wax which would allow changes to be made at a later stage if further information became available. The head was painted and fitted with glass eyes, which added greatly to its lifelike appearance. Hair and eyelashes were also provided, and the final result was a reasonably attractive young teenager. The hair, made from an inexpensive wig, was fitted for effect rather than accuracy. The head then became satisfactory for exhibition purposes. It is possible that a more authentically-styled coiffure will be provided at a later date. Additional colouring and make-up was kept to a minimum; so much time had been spent on producing the head that it seemed superfluous to colour it with heavy pigments round the eyes, although it is probable that more make-up would have been worn by this teenage girl when she was alive.

It is unlikely that it will ever be possible to make an absolutely accurate portrait of any individual from the skull alone, but it is possible to produce a head and a face of exact proportions, on which the relative positions of the eyes, nose, mouth, etc., are correctly related. Inevitably, there are areas where common sense assists a decision but by taking into account age, sex, build, and ethnic group, these reconstructions are far less speculative than might appear to be the case. Certainly, the head made for 1770 provides a far greater chance of relating the dried and fragmented remains to an actual person. She can now more readily be imagined laughing and crying, and perhaps suffering, if she lost her legs. This was the original objective when the project was started and to an extent it has been achieved.

FINGERPRINTS The unwrapping and fingerprint examination of the mummies, and in particular Asru, was of great interest to the police team involved in this project. There is plenty of evidence to show that for many centuries man had been interested in the configurations formed by the skin ridges on his fingers and palms, and in many societies a thumb print has been accepted in place of a signature; potters in Roman times left a print on the base of their work to show it was theirs. As you read this you are holding the book, and your prints will be left on the cover and on the pages as you turn over to read on.

If you look at the inner surface of your hand and touch the soles of your feet, you will find that the skin of these two areas is very different from the covering on the rest of your body. It is a hornier type of skin, taking the form of a system of minute skin ridges, roughly parallel with each other, changing direction here

and there while forming clearly defined patterns, particularly on the last joints of the fingers and thumbs. The ridges are called friction ridges. If you look again at your own fingers, you will see that these ridges are not continuous; there are frequent interruptions in their flow which are called ridge characteristics. A ridge may end suddenly in any direction, or it can fork into two diverse ridges; short independent ridges which lie between two others are a regular occurrence, and there may also be formations resembling lakes. All these are the more common type of characteristics, although there are others. All along the summits of the ridges and characteristics are microscopic pores which with others all over the body surface serve for the discharge of sweat from the body. When an article capable of retaining a finger mark is touched, an impression of the ridge detail and the characteristics may be left on it, in sweat. We can make this visible by the application of a suitable developer.

Mixing the paste before taking toe and finger prints of Asru

Above: A mould being
taken of the finger.
Right: An impression
being made of
the extremely well-
preserved toes

Our knowledge and continual research show that the friction
ridge surfaces are there from birth and persist throughout life.
Although the ridges, patterns, and characteristics are common to
all hands, no two impressions taken from different skin ridge
surfaces, whether they be from the same hand or from different
hands, have the same characteristics appearing in the same order
relative to each other. Because of this, identity can be established
by comparing fingerprints taken from a person with fingerprints
left elsewhere. While the task of the fingerprint officer is
normally to identify the criminal, it is often necessary to
fingerprint dead bodies in order to establish their identity.
These bodies may have been dead over a long period of time,
having frequently been recovered from water, and as a result the

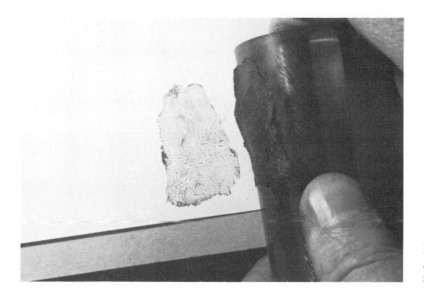

Left: A fingerprint of
Asru is obtained by
rolling the inked cast

flesh is putrefied and fragile. Nevertheless, there remains a
certain amount of flexibility in the fingers, and prints can be
obtained by conventional methods. In certain circumstances,
where the ridge surface is visible it is possible to record the
prints with the use of photography. The technique involves the
use of oblique lighting. This casts shadows from the ridges into
the depressions, thereby highlighting the ridges in contrast.
Similar effects were obtained when photographs were taken of
craters on the surface of the moon. Nobody, of course, was trying
to show that Asru had been a burglar, but nevertheless all the
knowledge we have outlined was brought into use when we
examined the mummy. Asru was not simply an ordinary dead
body. This meant that we had to use extreme care because of the
delicate rigidity of the flesh. The position of the hands excluded
the use of photography to record the prints, as there simply was
not enough room to position and manipulate a camera.

Up to now we have been talking mainly about fingerprints.
The palms, though, can provide certain information about a
person's activities during life; look at the hands of a man who
does manual work, feel the callouses, the thickened skin; then
look at the hands of, say, a clerk. He may have a small callous
where he holds his pen to write but the rest of his hand will be
relatively soft and unmarked. A man who dresses poultry may
have soft but strong hands; the softness will result from the fat
in a chicken's inside but the physical strength used in preparing
a bird for the oven ensures a firm, well-used hand.

Sole prints and toe prints can show not only deformity and
fungal infections, but also the damage which can` arise from
constantly walking barefoot. In the western world few of us
walk barefoot but in the past it was not always so. When it came

to dealing with Asru there was a very great difference between taking her fingerprints and those of a living person. In the case of the latter, one finger at a time is inked and then rolled in a special place on a pre-printed form. However, because Asru's fingers could not be moved for fear of damaging the delicate tissue, another method was needed. Fortunately, there is a special and very useful compound now in use in the dental profession. It combines at once a quick-setting quality with easy flexibility. We prepared small quantities of this compound, which looked very much like the putty used by a glazier. Then with one fingerprint officer holding Asru's delicate but rigid hand from the top, another officer carefully applied the grey compound to the surface of each finger, passing it gently upwards in the narrow space available. It was allowed a few moments to set, and was then carefully peeled away. The eight fingers and two thumbs were all treated in this way. Afterwards, several coats of black acrylic paint were applied to each of the moulds and then peeled away. These acrylic casts were inked and printed in the manner previously described.

These prints (page 181), as you will see if you compare them with your own, are not quite perfect because very small fragments of the mummified flesh are damaged. Nevertheless, their ridge characteristics are very clearly defined. A comparison of these shows that no fundamental change has occurred in the ridge system over the years. If Asru had been suspected of breaking into an Egyptian grocer's shop, and had left tell-tale marks, we have no doubt that we could produce suitable evidence. But there is no such imputation against the lady's character and we can let her rest in peace.

For the most part, fingerprint work involves comparing the prints of a suspect, taken in a police station, with the marks found at the scene of a crime. Sometimes the police have only the marks left at the scene of a crime and no trace of similar marks already on record. Then it is a matter of using years of experience to form a judgment. Frequently this judgment can be surprisingly accurate. For instance, experience can provide a reliable estimate of the age of a person leaving fingerprints. Although body cells are cast from the skin all the time and are replaced at the same rate, the texture of the ridges will be affected and the degree of wear and scarring will vary significantly. These features, if interpreted correctly, may lead to an estimation of age, a guide to the nature of occupation, and to general body structure. One recent example was that of a finger impression left behind at the scene of a murder. The opinion of the experts was that it had been made by a man aged between thirty-five and forty years, who did not do hard manual work and was fairly tall. When interviewed he turned out to be thirty-seven years of age, a hairdresser, five feet eleven inches tall.

So, with a view to working on these lines, we examined Asru's fingerprints and came to the conclusion that at the time of her death she was in her early forties. This estimate was later supported by evidence from other sources. It was also fairly clear that she did not do hard manual work. Her fingers had not met with the small accidents commonly encountered by a housewife looking after her home, or by a woman working in the fields. This type of work tends to crease the skin, to lessen the depth of the ridges, and to affect adversely the general condition of the skin.

With the idea of finding out whatever we could to assist in the general picture of Asru'a position in the world, we examined her toes. We took her toeprints in the same way that we had taken her fingerprints, by carefully applying the compound and allowing it to set before peeling it away. We applied the black acrylic paint to the mould to produce a positive cast. When the cast was inked we were able to examine in detail the features of the toeprints. Asru had been associated with the Temple of Karnak and she was entitled 'chantress of Amun'; that is, she was concerned with the chanting or singing of accompaniments to various temple rites. Some 3,000 years ago Egyptian temple dancers performed their ritual dances barefoot, the foot being used as part of the body's expression. The sole was in constant contact with the ground and even on the smoothest of flooring there would be friction and consequent wearing of the ridges on the underside of the toes and ball of the foot. Asru's feet did not show any traces of this constant contact with the floor, and the depth of the furrows and the clarity of the characteristics did not indicate that her role as chantress had also included the performance of ritual dances.

It is not often that such an unusual opportunity occurs for fingerprint officers to exercise their skills. Most of their working day is concerned with crime and those committing it. Look again at your own hand; the pattern of your fingerprints and the lines on your hand are unique to you. There is nobody quite like you in the whole world. This remains true for the burglar and for Asru, the temple chantress. This individuality can be identified throughout a whole spectrum of activities and has allowed us to explore the annals of history more thoroughly.

Epilogue

As DISCUSSED IN CHAPTER IV, the question arose as to whether mummy 1770 had been rewrapped at a much later date than the original embalming or death of the person involved. Dr G. W. A. Newton undertook the examination of the material from 1770 and the results by dating the bones and bandages are as follows:

	RADIOCARBON DATES		CALENDAR YEARS	
t½ years	5570	5730	5570	5730
	BP	BP	(tree-ring-corrected)	
Bones	3072	3161	1400 BC	1510 BC
	(plus or minus 150)			
Bandages	★ 1709	1758	270 AD	255 AD
	(plus or minus 150)			

(BP means before 1950)
(★Average of two separate determinations on bandages from different parts of the mummy)

As can be seen, this experiment showed very clearly that the age of the bones was far greater than had been suspected – somewhere between 1250 BC and 1600 BC – and that it was only the bandages which dated from between AD 105 and AD 405. While 1770 was being unwrapped, various inconsistencies and curious features had led the team to ask whether the mummy had been rewrapped after death. The clear indication from the results so far is that this had certainly happened up to seventeen hundred years after death. However it must be borne in mind that these results have been obtained on rather few specimens, and it is clearly important that further work be carried out to justify the conclusion.

Thus the Carbon-14 results made a very important contribution to the investigation of 1770 in that they provided an explanation for the most puzzling discrepancies which the evidence from this mummy provided when it was first unwrapped and which is described in detail on pages 88-101. The rewrapping of the body at a considerable length of time after its initial wrapping would explain its advanced state of decomposition at the time of the second wrapping, when very little skin tissue remained, some of the bones were missing, and there was complete absence of the internal organs. It would appear that the second wrapping was carried out on a body that had already considerably deteriorated.

A second wrapping would also explain why the resin was found present in some of the joints and between the bones of the spine, even though very little resin was found in the rest of the wrappings. The resin in the bones would have penetrated the body at the first embalment and wrapping.

It is apparent that because of the poor state of preservation of the body, the embalmers who carried out the rewrapping were unable to identify the person's sex and thus provided both gilded nipple amulets and a false phallus to equip the person for the afterlife.

Nevertheless, despite the lack of identification, the priests who performed the second wrapping treated the body as that of a high-ranking person, including artificial legs and feet to replace the missing limbs, beautifully decorated cartonnage sandals, and gilded finger-and toe-covers in addition to a fine cartonnage head mask and chest cover. Although the identity of the person was therefore unknown, it was perhaps the location in which the body was found which may have led the embalmers to assume that it was the body of a person of considerable importance, and this may have prompted them to rewrap the body in an elaborate manner. So, although the Carbon-14 results had provided answers to some of the most important questions, the conclusions now raised new queries regarding the identity and importance of the person. Unfortunately, it is almost certain that it will never be possible to supply the answers to these questions, because of the lack of inscriptional or other evidence.

In more general terms, the detailed examination of the group of mummies as a whole has provided interesting information regarding disease; some examples, such as the Guinea worm discovered in 1770, the presence of sand pneumoconiosis in the lung tissue of one of the Two Brothers, and the worm infestation found in the liver of Asru, were particularly noteworthy. Apart from the unusual condition of the teeth of 1770, the teeth of the other human mummies exhibited evidence of the same problems which seem to have afflicted many people in ancient Egypt. Although the cause of death is not apparent in most cases, some of the conditions mentioned above may well have hastened the death of an individual or brought it about.

The examination of these mummies has also assisted our knowledge of religious and funerary beliefs and customs,

Above and opposite:
The contrasting styles
of the two investigations.
Dr Murray in 1906
surrounded by members of
her medical team, and a
modern technician using
a light microscope
to examine rehydrated
mummified tissue

including the process of mummification, and of living conditions in ancient Egypt.

The other aim of the project was to establish a methodology, using many techniques under near-ideal conditions for the examination of a group of Egyptian mummified remains. This has proved especially worthwhile. The work on the Manchester project is now drawing to its conclusion. In addition to this book, inspired by the interest of the layman in the team's work, there has been a television programme, transmitted early in 1977 which was produced by the BBC in their *Chronicle* series; this dealt with the Mancester project against a background of Egyptian mummies and earlier investigations.

In addition, two short films, one showing the highlights in the procedure of unwrapping mummy 1770 and the other recording the various methods and techniques employed in examining all the Manchester mummies – are at present being produced by the audio-visual service of the University of Manchester, for general use in teaching departments.

The culmination of the team's work, however, will be the publication in the near future of a scientific book detailing the aims, techniques, and results of the processes carried out by the

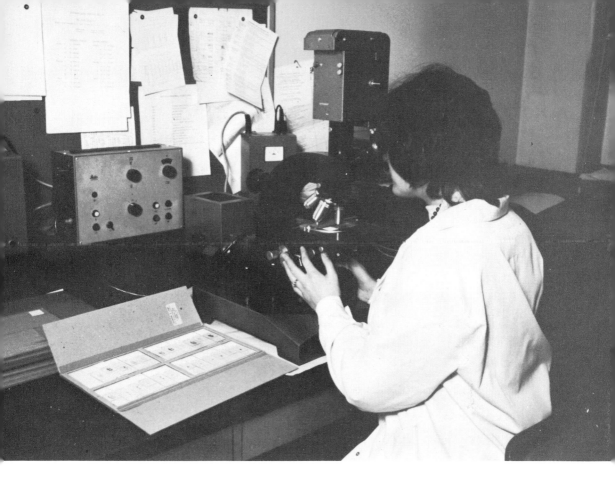

various specialists on the collection of human and animal mummies at the Manchester Museum. These results will then be related to the existing knowledge of living conditions, disease, and causes of death in ancient Egypt. Linked to this, an international symposium will shortly be held in Manchester entitled 'Science in Egyptology'; this will deal with the latest advances in the application of scientific and medical methods to the examination of Egyptian mummified remains.

The work of the project has been informative and even exciting. From the results at present available, it is apparent that future research in this field would add considerably to our knowledge of the ancient Egyptians in life and in death.

Contributors

The following members of the Manchester Mummy Team, listed alphabetically, contributed to *Mysteries of the Mummies*.

GEOFFREY G. BENSON MSc, PhD, MPS Lecturer in the Pharmacy Department, University of Manchester. Particular interests: pharmacognosy and phyto-chemistry.

A. CURRY BSc, PhD Senior Scientific Officer running an electron microscope unit for the Histopathology Department and public health laboratory at Withington Hospital. Work includes virus diagnosis and examination of renal disease and breast tumours. Doctoral thesis on the electron microscope structure of protozon, and first degree in Zoology from University of Manchester.

A. ROSALIE DAVID BA, PhD Took a degree in Egyptology at University College London and proceeded to a PhD on religious ritual in ancient Egyptian temples at University of Liverpool. At present she is Egyptologist at the Manchester Museum and Honorary Lecturer in Comparative Religion in the University of Manchester. Dr David has written books on Egyptian history and religion. Director of the Manchester Egyptian Mummy Research Project.

D. M. DIXON BA, PhD Lectures on Egyptology at University College London. Has worked on sites in Cyrenaica, Egypt, and the Sudan. His special interests are the environmental, social, and medical history of ancient Egypt, on which he has contributed papers to learned journals.

DETECTIVE CHIEF INSPECTOR A. FLETCHER Head of the Fingerprint Bureau and Scenes of Crime Department, Greater Manchester Police.

R. GARNER Worked originally in medical laboratory work, specializing in histology. Now on the technical staff in the natural history section of the Conservation Department at the Manchester Museum. Work involves preservation of new animal material and the conservation of existing specimens.

SARAH R. HEMINGWAY BSc, PhD, MPS of the University of Manchester is a lecturer in Pharmacy with a particular interest in pharmaceutical products of natural origin, including the isolation and identification of constituents of plant drugs.

PROFESSOR IAN ISHERWOOD MB, ChB, DMRD, FFR Professor of Diagnostic Radiology, University of Manchester. Consultant Neuroradiologist, Manchester Royal Infirmary.

HILARY M. JARVIS DCR Superintendent Radiographer in Department of Neuro-Radiology, The Royal Infirmary, Manchester.

F. N. LEACH MSc, PhD, MPS Qualified in pharmacy in 1962 and having worked in various branches of the profession entered medical research and was awarded a doctorate in 1973. Since then he has been responsible for the North-Western Regional Information Service on drugs.

F. F. LEEK LDS, RCS, FSA, FRGS Author of *The Human Remains from the Tomb of Tutankhamun* and many articles devoted to dentistry and Egyptology. During the last decade has visited Egypt and Sinai on ten occasions. He was a member of the team who examined the mummy of Tutankhamun in 1967, and has appeared in several BBC television films concerned with ancient Egypt.

R. A. H. NEAVE FMAA, AIMBI Studied at the Hastings School of Art and the Middlesex Hospital, London. Joined the University of Manchester in 1959 as a Medical Artist.

G. W. A. NEWTON BSc, PhD, CChem, MRIC Senior Lecturer in Department of Chemistry, University of Manchester. Specially interested in Carbon-14 dating techniques Dr Newton has set up a Carbon-14 dating Unit at Manchester.

E. TAPP MD, MRC Path, MRCS Eng, LRCP Lond Qualified MBChB in Liverpool, and proceeded to MD (Liverpool). Became member of the Royal College of Pathologists in 1968. Previously Consultant in Histopathology and Morbid Anatomy at the University Hospital of South Manchester and Honorary Lecturer in Pathology at the University of Manchester. Now holds similar posts at the Group Laboratory, Preston Royal Infirmary.

Editorial Consultant: James Forde-Johnston, Keeper of Ethnology at the Manchester University Museum.

Acknowledgments

We should like to express our thanks to the following for their support and co-operation.

The University of Manchester, the Chairman and members of the Manchester Museum Committee, and the Director of the Museum. Dr A. J. N. W. Prag and other members of the curatorial staff, Mrs C. M. Higginbottom, the Superintendent, and members of the technical staff of the Museum, especially in the areas of photography, conservation, drawing, and joinery. The British Academy for a grant towards our research, and Kodak Ltd. for a most generous supply of film. To the staff of various departments and institutions of the University, including Dr F. B. Beswick, Executive Dean of the Medical School, Mr F. Silvo, and members of staff of the Medical School; Mr L. Lawler, Director of the Audio-Visual Service, Mr K. Wrench, Producer, and the staff of the department; Mr P. Radcliffe, Head of Communications, and the staff of the Communications Office; Miss R. McGuinness and the staff of the Dental School; Miss E. McCauley, Dept. of Pharmacy; Dr C. A. Shuttleworth and Mrs J. L. Ward, Dept. of Medical Biochemistry; Mr M. Ashworth, Dept. of Medicine; Professor W. MacKenzie, Dept. of Geology; the Dept. of Zoology for use of transport. To the staff of the Departments of Neuro-radiology and Anatomy at Manchester Royal Infirmary, and to the Director and staff of the Department of Medical Illustration at that hospital. To Mr K. Hollins, Senior Chief Technician at Withington Hospital, and his team of histology technicians at that hospital; Mr K. Hodge who carried out most of the measurements for the Carbon-14 dates; Mr R. White for preliminary radiography at the Museum; Dr J. P. Wilde for advice on textiles; Dr O. Amit for an authentic sample of Dead Sea bitumen; Mr G. Irving; Mrs J. Ovenden. To the Flinders Petrie Museum, University College, London; Mr P. Jordan and Miss A. Benson Gyles, and members of the BBC *Chronicle* team. Finally, the team would like to thank Book Club Associates for their encouragement and enthusiasm throughout the production of this book.

Illustration acknowledgments

The publishers wish to thank the following for granting permission to use their illustrations.

AEI Scientific Apparatus Ltd: p. 137. Dr A. Curry: pp. 146, 161, 163, 164, 165. Dr A. Rosalie David: pp. 29, 30, 32, 33, 49, 50. Department of Medical Illustration, Withington Hospital: p. 140. Shaun Edwards: p. 176. R. Garner: pp. 72, 73. Greater Manchester Police: pp. 179, 180, 181. Michael Holford Library: pp. 10/11, 12, 14, 17, 18, 20, 21, 24, 27, 35, 36, 38, 39, 44/45. Professor Ian Isherwood: pp. 108, 111, 112, 113, 116, 117, 120, 121, 122, 124, 125, 126, 127. Lancashire Area Health Authority: pp. 99, 128, 131, 133, 142, 145. Dr F. N. Leach: pp. 102, 103, 104, 105. F. F. Leek: pp. 65, 148, 151, 153, 154. Manchester Museum: pp. 8, 9, 41, 48, 52, 54, 55, 57, 59, 62, 66, 69, 77, 80, 139, 158. Dr E. Tapp: pp. 2, 6, 82, 84, 86, 89, 90, 91, 92, 93, 94, 96. University Hospital of South Manchester, Department of Medical Illustration: p. 187. University of Manchester: p. 186. University of Manchester, Department of Medical Illustration: pp. 157, 169, 171, 172, 173, 174, 175, 177.

Map on p. 15 by A. R. Garrett.

Index